Light for the Journey

A FRESH FOCUS ON DOCTRINE

A. D. BEACHAM, JR.

LifeSprings Resources
P.O. Box 9
Franklin Springs, GA 30639-0009

Light for the Journey: A Fresh Focus on Doctrine
© 1998 by A. D. Beacham, Jr.

2nd Edition November, 2000.

Scripture references quote the New King James Version in the *Spirit-Filled Life Bible* (Thomas Nelson Publishers, Nashville), unless otherwise indicated.

All rights reserved. No part of this book may be reproduced, stored in a retrieval system, or transmitted in any form or by any means—for example, electronic, mechanical, photocopy, record, or any other—without the prior permission of the publisher.

Published by LifeSprings Resources
P.O. Box 9
Franklin Springs, Georgia, 30639

Printed in the United States of America
ISBN: 0-91186-6418

Library of Congress-Cataloging in Publication Data

Contents

Introduction 5

Lesson 1: **Who Is God?** 7

Lesson 2: **Who Is Jesus Christ?** 15

Lesson 3: **Who Is the Holy Spirit?** 23

Lesson 4: **The Holy Scriptures** 31

Lesson 5: **Human Destiny** 41

Lesson 6: **The Meaning of Salvation** 49

Lesson 7: **Justified by Faith** 57

Lesson 8: **Sanctification** 67

Lesson 9: **The Pentecostal Experience** ... 77

Lesson 10: **Living in the Spirit** 85

Lesson 11: **Divine Healing** 93

Lesson 12: **Christ's Second Coming** 101

Lesson 13: **The Meaning and Mission of the Church** 109

Introduction

This elective study provides you a contemporary way of reflecting on the great truths of the Christian faith. Using as a basis the Fourteen Articles of Faith of the International Pentecostal Holiness Church, this study can be used by any local congregation, denomination, or charismatic group that affirms these biblical truths.

Someone might say, "theology is boring." That's not true. Sometimes preachers, teachers, and writers are boring; but not theology. Theology is God doing "God-talk" to us. Taken from the Word of God, the Bible, theology tells us the truth about our sinful condition, God's divine remedy in Jesus Christ, and the glory of God's love and righteousness.

The practice of the early church is instructive. Almost all apostolic letters began with theology and then made practical application of divine truth to local situations. The same is true for the effective church in century 21. It will be a church whose theology is biblically based, communicated clearly, and applied with integrity and love.

A theology teacher who taught me much in and since seminary, wrote that "the renewal of the church rests upon two foundations. The first is the renewal of faith, the outpouring of the Holy Spirit that enables us to say that Jesus is the Christ, that enables us to experience the Bible as the Word of God, that makes us sensitive to the activity of God in nature and in history. The second foundation is the act of remembering and recovering our identity and persuasively proclaiming it in the life of the church..."[1]

That has been the goal of Shirley Spencer and me in preparing the outlines upon which these lessons are written. This study has been prepared in response to a growing chorus calling for ancient biblical truths to be presented in a contemporary format. While acknowledging that all such efforts can be improved, it is our prayer that you will find these lessons informative and useful in helping you grow as disciples of Jesus Christ. Our prayer for you is found in Hebrews 10:23, "Let us hold fast the confession of our hope without wavering, for He who promised is faithful"; and 2 Timothy 3:16, 17, "All Scripture is given by inspiration of God, and is profitable for doctrine, for reproof, for correction, for instruction in righteousness, that the man of God may be complete, thoroughly equipped for every good work."

Doug Beacham
Franklin Springs, Georgia

Shirley Spencer
Oklahoma City, Oklahoma

Spring, 1998

ENDNOTES

1. John H. Leith, *From Generation to Generation: The Renewal of the Church According to Its Own Theology and Practice,* John Knox Press, Westminster, Louisville, KY, 1990, pp. 15, 16.

Lesson 1

Who Is God?

Faith Declaration

We believe there is but one living and true God everlasting, of infinite power, wisdom and goodness; Maker and Preserver of all things, both visible and invisible. And in the unity of this Godhead, there are three Persons of one substance of eternal being, and equal in holiness, justice, wisdom, power, and dignity; the Father, the Son, and the Holy Ghost.

Bible Focus

"I am the Lord, that is My name; And My glory I will not give to another, Nor My praise to carved images." —Isaiah 42:8

Lesson Objective

To better understand who God is and worship Him.

Global Outreach Emphasis

Christians are called to demonstrate God's love to the world.

What's This Lesson About?

God. Gott. Deus. Dieu. Dios. Theos. Elohim. Onyame. Mungu. Oluwa. Allah.[1] People worldwide recognize and give name to that Someone who is above all. Men and women stand amazed at the expanse of stars, raging storms, beautiful sunsets, majestic mountains, and the birth of a child. They know there is a Creator, God (Romans 1:20; Psalm 19:1-6). But how do we personally know "God"?

For 250 years, Western thought has left modern man questioning the existence of God. Is God nothing more than a projection of man, as Feuerbach proposed in the nineteenth century? Is God a convenient excuse to protect the interest of the bourgeoisie, as Marx proposed? Is God an infantile illusion, as Freud proposed?[2]

Or is God the Creator, Sustainer, and Redeemer of the universe? Evangelical, Spirit-filled Christians believe that God does exist and that what the Bible says of Him is true. This is because the Bible is God's own revelation to us of what we need to know of His character and purposes.[3]

The Faith Declaration gives us three important aspects of the nature of God vital for a biblical and living faith in this generation: 1. Monotheism; 2. God is love; 3. The Triune nature of God.

1. God Is One
(Deuteronomy 6:4, 5)

Deuteronomy 6:4 Hear, O Israel: The Lord our God, the Lord is one!

5 You shall love the Lord your God with all your heart, with all your soul, and with all your strength.

Christianity, along with Judaism and Islam, is one of the three great monotheistic religions. Christians believe there is but one living and true God. Christians do not believe there are many gods with one supreme God. Christians do not believe that Satan is a god nor that Satan is of equal power with God (Deuteronomy 4:35; Isaiah 44:6, 8).

Christian belief derives from Hebrew faith. Abraham, Isaac, and Jacob are forefathers of faith for Gentiles who have accepted Jesus as Israel's Messiah. Thus, the Old Testament is an indispensable part of Christian faith.

Deuteronomy 6:4 is the central Hebrew confession of faith. It is known as the "Shema," because *Shema* is the first Hebrew word of the confession and means "hear." God gave Israel the truth concerning Himself when He called her to listen and know that "the Lord thy God is one." That is why the Ten Commandments begin with warnings about idolatry (Exodus 20:1-6; Deuteronomy 5:6-10). Israel's great prophets had to continually rebuke the people for disobeying these commandments and worshiping other gods, which were not gods at all (Isaiah 2:8, 17, 20, 21; 40:18-23, 25; 44:6-8; Jeremiah 2:4, 5; 10:1-10). Jesus taught the Shema as affirming the eternal truth that there is but One God (Mark 12:29).

2. God Is Love
(1 John 4:7-21)

1 John 4:7 Beloved, let us love one another, for love is of God; and everyone who loves is born of God and knows God.

8 He who does not love does not know God, for God is love.

9 In this the love of God was manifested toward us, that God has sent His only begotten Son into the world, that we might live through Him.

10 In this is love, not that we loved God, but that He loved us and sent His Son to be the propitiation for our sins.

11 Beloved, if God so loved us, we also ought to love one another.

12 No one has seen God at any time. If we love one another, God abides in us, and His love has been perfected in us.

13 By this we know that we abide in Him, and He in us, because He has given us of His Spirit.

14 And we have seen and testify that the Father has sent the Son as Savior of the world.

15 Whoever confesses that Jesus is the Son of God, God abides in him, and he in God.

16 And we have known and believed the love that God has for us. God is love, and he who abides in love abides in God, and God in him.

17 Love has been perfected among us in this: that we may have boldness in the day of judgment; because as He is, so are we in this world.

18 There is no fear in love; but perfect love casts out fear, because fear involves torment. But he who fears has not been made perfect in love.

19 We love Him because He first loved us.

20 If someone says, "I love God," and hates his brother, he is a liar; for he who does not love his brother whom he has seen, how can he love God whom he has not seen?

21 And this commandment we have from Him: that he who loves God must love his brother also.

How do you describe God? Scripture's greatest description is that God is love. "Love is the very essence of the divine nature," writes J. Rodman Williams.[4] The statement, "God is love," means that God is not an impersonal force but that He is personal and can be known as He reveals Himself. "God is love" means that God is in eternal relationship with Himself (through the Son and the Holy Spirit). "God is love" means that God is in relationship with what He has created. "God is love" is the foundation for divine goodness, the redemption of sinful humanity, and the ultimate restoration of this fallen world.

Chesed is the primary Old Testament word and *agape* is the primary New Testament word revealing God's love to us. These words denote covenant love that is based on God's unchanging Word and character. God is faithful because He keeps His Word. God is just because His Word reflects His love. God is righteous because His actions are always in perfect love and truth.

Christians can be assured of God's loving kindness and care because His actions are consistent with that revelation. Even His wrath and discipline are expressions of His love and determination that sin will not frustrate His eternal purposes for us in Christ Jesus.

3. One God–Three Persons
(Matthew 3:16, 17; 28:19; 2 Corinthians 13:14; 1 John 5:7)

Matthew 3:16 When He had been baptized, Jesus came up immediately from the water; and behold, the heavens were opened to Him, and He saw the Spirit of God descending like a dove and alighting upon Him.

17 And suddenly a voice came from heaven, saying, "This is My beloved Son, in whom I am well pleased."

28:19 Go therefore and make disciples of all the nations, baptizing them in the name of the Father and of the Son and of the Holy Spirit.

2 Corinthians 13:14 The grace of the Lord Jesus Christ, and the love of God, and the communion of the Holy Spirit be with you all. Amen.

1 John 5:7 For there are three that bear witness in heaven: the Father, the Word, and the Holy Spirit; and these three are one.

Millions of Christians sing Reginal Heber's words, "Holy, holy, holy! ... God in three Persons, blessed Trinity!" The Christian doctrine of the Trinity is not a man-made effort to understand God. As the above texts show, this doctrine is revealed in Scripture. The church, through its councils and creeds, has come to an understanding of Scripture that has passed the test of time and maintains the vital truths of God's triune nature, truths necessary for our salvation.

The lesson began with a reference to the Hebrew name for God, *Elohim*. This plural name denotes the reality of God's personhood as revealed in the Bible. Referring to Genesis 1:26, Martin Luther wrote that the phrase "Let Us" in reference to God, "is aimed at making sure the mystery of our faith, by which we believe that from eternity there is one God and that there are three separate Persons in one Godhead: the Father, the Son, and the Holy Spirit."[5] Referring to the use of *Elohim* in Genesis 11:7, Luther maintained, "that there is a plurality in God characterized by an undivided essence and an inseparable unity."[6] From the New Testament and insights gained through centuries of orthodox Christian thought, we discover the following truths about the Trinity:

The Father, Son, and Holy Spirit have coexisted from eternity. The Son, Jesus Christ, is not a created being, but is begotten of the Father from eternity.

The Father, Son, and Holy Spirit are divine and worthy of worship either together or, from the limitations of human understanding, separately as we focus on the specific benefits provided by each.

The Christian doctrine of the Trinity reveals that divine love and divine communication have eternally existed in the unique and eternal relationship of the Father, the Son, and the Holy Spirit. This means that God, in His fullness, is able to communicate with us and show His love to us.[7]

Global Outreach Emphasis
Christians are called to demonstrate God's love to the world.
1 John 4:7-21 reveals a close link between the reality of God's love and a Christian's love for others. As people redeemed by Christ, we are commanded to love our neighbors and our enemies, and a husband is commanded to love his wife as Christ loved the church. Thus, "God is love" is not mere talk. It is the foundation for genuine and fulfilling human relationships.

Who is God? He is the Triune One who loves His creation. He is the Triune One who has come to save lost humanity. He is the Triune One whose Spirit is mightily working today.

Word Power
GOD'S NATURE AND ATTRIBUTES
Scripture reveals to us many important truths concerning God. Besides being One, God is also living (Joshua 3:10; John 6:57), true (John 17:3), everlasting (Isaiah 40:28; Romans 1:20), and Spirit (John 4:24: Colossians 1:15).

The Bible often uses human metaphors to describe God's actions, such as the "arm" of the Lord, etc. This is called anthropomorphism and is God's accommodation in communicating to us so we can understand Him. God does not have a human body (except for the brief years that Jesus was in the flesh). Genesis 1:26 indicates that humans are made in God's image. In light of the total witness of Scripture, that means we are created in God's spiritual and moral image.

God is neither male nor female. These are human sexual distinctions for earth-bound life. God reveals Himself as "Father" in order to manifest genuine protection, provision, and care. The "Fatherhood of God" is not a man-made concept conditioned by culture but rather God's own self-revelation as a witness to humanity of this aspect of His character.

Noel Brooks writes of the attributes of God in three general categories: 1. *God's physical attributes,* which include His omnipotence (Genesis 17:1; Revelation 19:6) and omnipresence (Jeremiah 23:23, 24; Psalm 139:7-10); 2. *God's intellectual attributes,* which include infinite wisdom (Psalm 104:24; Daniel 2:20, 21; Colossians 2:2, 3) and omniscience (Hebrews 4:13; Isaiah 40:28); 3. *God's moral attributes,* which include goodness (Psalm 106:1; Matthew 5:44, 45), righteousness (Psalm 99:4; John 17:25), faithfulness (Numbers 23:19; 2 Timothy 2:13), holiness (Exodus 15:11; 1 Peter 1:15, 16), mercy (Exodus 34:6; Psalm 103:4, 8), love (John 3:16; Romans 5:8), and grace (Ephesians 1:6, 7; Titus 2:11).[8]

ENDNOTES

1. English, German, Latin, French, Spanish, Greek, Hebrew, Twi (Ghana), Swahili (Kenya), Yoruba (Nigeria), Arabic. These names refer to the Christian God. Arabic-speaking Christians use the name Allah in reference to God as revealed by the Bible.

2. Hans Kung, *Does God Exist? An Answer for Today,* Vintage Books, New York, 1981, pp. 191-337.

3. Refer to Lesson 4 for insights regarding the Bible as the Word of God.

4. J. Rodman Williams, *Renewal Theology: God, the World & Redemption,* Volume 1, Academic Books, a division of Zondervan Publishing House, Grand Rapids, Michigan, 1988, p. 63. Williams gives the following aspects of "God is love": 1. "It is the nature of God to love"; 2. "The love of God is spontaneous. God loves because love is His very nature"; 3. "God's love is never self-seeking but always self-giving"; 4. "The content of the divine love can be apprehended only in God's action"; 5. "The love of God is unfathomable" (p. 65).

5. Martin Luther, *Luther's Works*, Vol. 1, *Lectures on Genesis Chapters 1-5*, edited by Jaroslav Pelikan, Concordia Publishing House, St. Louis, 1958, p. 57.

6. Martin Luther, *Luther's Works*, Vol. 2, *Lectures on Genesis Chapters 6-14*, edited by Jaroslav Pelikan, Concordia Publishing House, St. Louis, 1958, p. 227. (It should also be noted that the Trinity is revealed in Isaiah 6:8.)

7. Francis Schaeffer has an insightful discussion of this in *Genesis in Time and Space.*

8. Noel Brooks, *The Pentecostal Holiness Advocate*, January 3, 1970, p. 13.

Lesson 2

Who Is Jesus Christ?

Faith Declaration

We believe that the Son, who is the Word of the Father, the very and eternal God, of one substance with the Father, took man's nature in the womb of the blessed virgin; so that two whole and perfect natures, that is to say, the Godhead and the manhood were joined together in one Person, never to be divided, whereof is one Christ, very God and perfect man, who actually suffered, was crucified, dead, and buried, to reconcile the Father to us, and to make atonement, not only for our actual guilt, but also for original sin.

We believe that Christ did truly rise again from the dead, and took again His body, with all things appertaining to the perfections of man's nature, and ascended into heaven and there sits until He shall return to judge all men at the last day.

Bible Focus

"Jesus said … 'I am the way, the truth, and the life. No one comes to the Father except through Me.'" —John 14:6

Lesson Objective

To better understand who Jesus Christ is and seek to know Him.

Global Outreach Emphasis

Jesus Christ, God's only begotten Son, came to seek and save the lost.

What's This Lesson About?

Jesus Christ. There's just something about that name! Look at the majesty and power found in that name: *Jesus* is Greek for the Hebrew word *Joshua,* meaning *The Lord is Savior; Christ* is the Greek for the Hebrew title *Messiah,* meaning *Anointed One.*

The modern world offers its interpretations of Christ through Andrew Lloyd-Webber and Tim Rice's *Jesus Christ Superstar* and Nikos Kazantzakis' *The Last Temptation of Christ.* Christian writers present Him as Aslan, the Lion-King of C. S. Lewis' *The Chronicles of Narnia,* and Prince Myshkin in Dostoyevsky's insightful *The Idiot.* But the Bible informs us who Jesus Christ is by giving us enough information to comprehend the divine plan of salvation and the role He has in that plan as the eternal Son of God.

"We cannot vex the devil more than by teaching, preaching, singing, and talking of Jesus," said Martin Luther.[1] The old hymn reminds us that "Jesus is the the sweetest name I know." His name comforts and encourages us and vexes the devil. There *is* just something about that name!

1. Son of God
(Psalm 2:7, 8; Mark 1:9-11;
1 John 2:18, 21-23; 5:4, 5, 10-13, NKJV)

Psalm 2:7 I will declare the decree: The Lord has said to Me, "You are My Son, Today I have begotten You.
8 Ask of Me, and I will give You The nations for Your inheritance, And the ends of the earth for Your possession."

Mark 1:9 It came to pass in those days that Jesus came from Nazareth of Galilee, and was baptized by John in the Jordan.

10 And immediately, coming up from the water, He saw the heavens parting and the Spirit descending upon Him like a dove.

11 Then a voice came from heaven, "You are My beloved Son, in whom I am well pleased."

1 John 2:18 Little children, it is the last hour; and as you have heard that the Antichrist is coming, even now many antichrists have come, by which we know that it is the last hour.

21 I have not written to you because you do not know the truth, but because you know it, and that no lie is of the truth.

22 Who is a liar but he who denies that Jesus is the Christ? He is antichrist who denies the Father and the Son.

23 Whoever denies the Son does not have the Father either; he who acknowledges the Son has the Father also.

5:4 For whatever is born of God overcomes the world. And this is the victory that has overcome the world—our faith.

5 Who is he who overcomes the world, but he who believes that Jesus is the Son of God?

10 He who believes in the Son of God has the witness in himself; he who does not believe God has made Him a liar, because he has not believed the testimony that God has given of His Son.

11 And this is the testimony: that God has given us eternal life, and this life is in His Son.

12 He who has the Son has life; he who does not have the Son of God does not have life.

13 These things I have written to you who believe in the name of the Son of God, that you may know that you have eternal life, and that you may continue to believe in the Son of God.

Salvation rests upon the reality that Jesus of Nazareth was the incarnate Son of God. The virgin birth affirms that Jesus was born without the stain of original sin and that He was the eternal Son of the Father. Jesus came to this earth in fulfillment of the eternal plan to save lost humanity.

Through the Bible, God has always shown us these truths concerning the person of His Son. Old Testament saints had a glimpse of the truth that unfolded in the birth and ministry of Jesus. The Father affirmed His pleasure and delight in the ministry of His Son at the baptism in the Jordan River.

John's letter shows the importance of the confession that Jesus is the Son of God. The denial of this truth is part of the spirit of antichrist. We see this in our day with teachings denying this unique relationship between Jesus and the heavenly Father. If you confess that Jesus is the Son of God, then all other world religions stand under divine judgment as inadequate for salvation. If you deny that Jesus is the Son of God, then you lower Christianity to equal, or less than equal, status with humanity's efforts to save itself.

This confession is so significant that John declares that one cannot deny that Jesus is the Son of God and be a Christian. This remains a clear point of truth for Christians today. Regardless of intentions, those who deny the Sonship of Jesus are under the influence of the spirit of antichrist and only serve to confuse and destroy the souls of many.

2. Son of Man
(Daniel 7:13, 14; Mark 9:31; 10:45)

Daniel 7:13 I was watching in the night visions, And behold, One like the Son of Man, Coming with the clouds of heaven! He came to the Ancient of Days, And they brought Him near before Him.

14 Then to Him was given dominion and glory and a kingdom, That all peoples, nations, and languages should serve

Him. His dominion is an everlasting dominion, Which shall not pass away, And His kingdom the one Which shall not be destroyed.

Mark 9:31 For He taught His disciples and said to them, "The Son of Man is being betrayed into the hands of men, and they will kill Him. And after He is killed, He will rise the third day."

Mark 10:45 For even the Son of Man did not come to be served, but to serve, and to give His life a ransom for many.

Jesus fulfills many of the promises and types found in the Old Testament, including the Son of Man. As the Daniel passage shows, the Son of Man is the eschatological figure who will appear at the end of the age ushering in the age of God's kingdom.

Jesus took that prophetic role, dimly visible to Daniel, and added two special dimensions to the majesty and power of the coming King of kings. The first was that the Son of Man would suffer, die, and be raised from the dead. Jesus combined the suffering servant of Isaiah 53 with that of the majestic Son of Man in Daniel. This revealed that the Lord of the universe paid the price to redeem sinful man. The second dimension is found in those sayings reflecting the humanity of the Son of Man. The ministry of the Son of Man is more than a cosmic event; it includes the personal application of forgiveness to those who hear and respond to His voice with confession and repentance.

3. Savior of the World
(Isaiah 19:20; Matthew 1:21; John 4:42)

Isaiah 19:20 And it will be for a sign and for a witness to the Lord of hosts in the land of Egypt; for they will cry to the Lord because of the oppressors, and He will send them a Savior and a Mighty One, and He will deliver them.

Matthew 1:21 And she will bring forth a Son, and you shall call His name Jesus, for He will save His people from their sins.

John 4:42 Then they said to the woman, "Now we believe, not because of what you said, for we ourselves have heard Him and we know that this is indeed the Christ, the Savior of the world."

Jesus, the eternal Son of God, the revealed Son of Man, the Christ (Messiah) of Israel, is the Savior of the world. There is no other name or person in heaven or earth who has paid the price for human redemption from sin. Only God could pay that price of appeasing His righteous wrath and releasing His holy love to us through the blood of His only Son, Jesus. This is the good news of the gospel: Jesus came to save sinners. This means that our Creator has rightfully diagnosed the terminal condition of sinful man, and the only sufficient cure has been applied by and through the blood of our Redeemer, Jesus the Savior.

Global Outreach Emphasis

Jesus Christ, God's only begotten Son, came to seek and save the lost. What is our motivation for world evangelism? The fact is that God loved the world so much that He sent His Son to a lost and dying world. Just as the love of God was the source of the Son's leaving the glory of heaven and traveling to our distant world, so also God's love compels us to do our part in going the distance for the lost around us.

We must be willing to become a church without walls to those different in race, language, and customs. We must be willing to give generously and, if called, to travel to distant shores for the cause of the Savior. World evangelism is not a Christian option; it is the heart of the Savior put into action by our obedience.

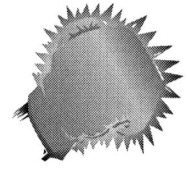

Word Power
CHRIST'S WORK AS PROPITIATION

"Our salvation rests on two great truths. First, on the Person of the Saviour Himself, the Son of God, the Son of Man, whose name is Jesus; and secondly, on the work He has wrought. These are inseparably connected together in the Word of God, and we cannot rightly receive the one without the other," so wrote Henry Soltau, a nineteenth-century English clergyman.[2] The confession described in the Faith Declaration, like several in this study, is from the Thirty-Nine Articles of Religion of the Church of England. While some of the phrasing is slightly different (without changing the theological intention of the Thirty-Nine Articles), these faith declarations are rooted in biblical and historical theological reflection.

The truths affirmed in the Thirty-Nine Articles and in the Faith Declaration concerning Jesus Christ are based on truths affirmed in the Apostles' and Nicene Creeds, and the Council at Chalcedon (dating from the second, fourth and fifth centuries). These creeds affirm the central part of the preaching of the early church (1 Corinthians 15:3, 4). It is important to note that the Faith Declaration affirmed clear reasons why Christ died, "to reconcile the Father to us, and to make atonement, not only for our actual guilt, but also for original sin." Why did Christ have "to reconcile the Father to us"? In the Edwardian Homilies of 1547, a series of twelve sermons written by Thomas Cranmer, this leader of the English Reformation wrote that Christ came into this world "to fulfill the law for us, and, by shedding of his most precious blood, to make a sacrifice and satisfaction, or (as it may be called) amends to his Father for our sins, to assuage his wrath and indignation conceived against us for the same."[2]

The action of Christ in reconciling the Father to us is called propitiation. This refers to the mercy seat, or lid, of the Ark of the Covenant and the blood of the sacrifice which was sprinkled upon it to appease God's wrath and atone for sin (Exodus 25:17-22; Leviticus 16:2, 11-15; Hebrews 9:5; 2:17; Romans 3:25; 1 John 2:2; 4:10). God's wrath against sin is righteous because His law is holy. We are deserving of wrath because we have broken God's law by our sins. God could not ignore His law and simply say, "I forgive you." That would be contrary to His holy nature and cheapen the blood of Christ. The fact that God's wrath was appeased by the blood of the sacrifice means that we can be certain that the price has been paid for our redemption and that God's offer of forgiveness is absolutely trustworthy. The blood of Jesus is the price that propitiates God's righteous anger and pays for our atonement from sin. In this way, the Father is reconciled to us, and we, being reconciled to Him, are reconciled to one another and by holy lives show the world this "ministry of reconciliation" (2 Corinthians 5:18).

ENDNOTES

1. Thomas S. Kepler, ed., *The Table Talk of Martin Luther*, Baker Book House, Grand Rapids, 1952, p. 106.

2. Henry W. Soltau, *The Tabernacle, The Priesthood, and The Offerings*, Christian Publications, Inc., Harrisburg, Pennsylvania, 1965 reprint, p. 142.

3. John H. Leith, ed., *Creeds of the Churches,* Doubleday Anchor, New York, 1963, p. 240.

Lesson 3

Who Is the Holy Spirit?

Faith Declaration

We believe the Holy Ghost, proceeding from the Father and the Son, is of one substance, majesty and glory with the Father and the Son, very and eternal God.

Bible Focus

"When the Helper comes, whom I shall send to you from the Father, the Spirit of truth who proceeds from the Father, He will testify of Me." —John 15:26

Lesson Objective

To better understand who the Holy Spirit is and seek His fellowship.

Global Outreach Emphasis

The Holy Spirit leads sinners to saving faith in Jesus Christ.

What's This Lesson About?

Bishop Joseph A. Synan wrote that "the Holy Ghost—or Holy Spirit—is a person and that He is the executive agent of the Godhead in the dispensation of grace; that He anoints the preaching of the Word, convicts of sin and applies the benefits of the atonement; that He is our Teacher, Comforter, and Guide, taking the things of Christ and revealing them to us, glorifying Christ, guiding us into all truth, and showing us things to come; that all of these ministries are based upon and function in accordance with the written Word of God."[1]

In this era of the Spirit, it is exciting to explore the rich biblical material regarding the person and work of the Holy Spirit. The person and work of the Holy Spirit are more than just speaking in tongues or other charismatic gifts (these ministries will be discussed in Lessons 9 and 10). In this lesson, we discover the wonderful presence and work of the Holy Spirit in creation and God's redemptive purposes in the world.

1. Spirit of God
(Genesis 1:2; Isaiah 11:1, 2; John 4:23, 24; Acts 13:1-4)

Genesis 1:2 The earth was without form, and void; and darkness was on the face of the deep. And the Spirit of God was hovering over the face of the waters.

Isaiah 11:1 There shall come forth a Rod from the stem of Jesse, And a Branch shall grow out of his roots.

2 The Spirit of the Lord shall rest upon Him, The Spirit of wisdom and understanding, The Spirit of counsel and might, The Spirit of knowledge and of the fear of the Lord.

John 4:23 But the hour is coming, and now is, when the true worshipers will worship the Father in spirit and truth; for the Father is seeking such to worship Him.

24 God is Spirit, and those who worship Him must worship in spirit and truth.

Acts 13:1 Now in the church that was at Antioch there were certain prophets and teachers: Barnabas, Simeon who was called Niger, Lucius of Cyrene, Manaen who had been brought up with Herod the tetrarch, and Saul.

2 As they ministered to the Lord and fasted, the Holy Spirit said, "Now separate to Me Barnabas and Saul for the work to which I have called them."

3 Then, having fasted and prayed, and laid hands on them, they sent them away.

4 So, being sent out by the Holy Spirit, they went down to Seleucia, and from there they sailed to Cyprus.

The Holy Spirit is the Spirit of God and is worthy of our worship. As divine personality, He has intelligence, will, sensitivity (1 Corinthians 2:10, 11; 12:11; Acts 15:28; Matthew 12:31). This means He is personal and is not an impersonal "force" or "power," although He has power. As a real person, the Holy Spirit can be grieved and resisted by unbelievers and believers (Acts 7:51; Ephesians 4:30). As divine wisdom, He was active in the creation of the world (Genesis 1:2; Proverbs 8:22-31).

The words *ruach* (Hebrew) and *pneuma* (Greek) can also be translated "breath, wind." Like the wind, the Spirit of God blows and cannot be controlled by human effort. As R. A. Torrey writes, "The Spirit like the wind is invisible but none the less perceptible and real and mighty."[2]

There are numerous Scriptural names of the Holy Spirit that further reveal His person and work: "the Spirit of the Living God" (2 Corinthians 3:3), "the Spirit of Christ" (Romans 8:9), "the Spirit of Jesus Christ" (Philippians 1:19), "the Spirit of Jesus" (Acts 16:6, 7), "the Spirit of His Son" (Galatians 4:6), "the Holy Spirit of promise" (Ephesians 1:13), "the Spirit of holiness" (Romans 1:4), "the Spirit of judgment" and "the

Spirit of burning" (Isaiah 4:4), "the Spirit of truth" (John 14:17), "the Spirit of life" (Romans 8:2), "the oil of gladness" (Hebrews 1:9), "the Spirit of grace" (Hebrews 10:29), "the Spirit of glory" (1 Peter 4:14).

Just as Jesus is a distinct person in the Godhead yet is one with the Father, so also the Holy Spirit is a distinct person in the Godhead yet is one with the Father and Son. The Holy Spirit is eternal in existence with the Father and Son.

2. God's Presence in the World
(Isaiah 61:1-3; John 14:16, 17, 25, 26; 15:26; 16:5-15; 1 Corinthians 6:9)

Isaiah 61:1 The Spirit of the Lord God is upon Me, Because the Lord has anointed Me To preach good tidings to the poor; He has sent Me to heal the brokenhearted, To proclaim liberty to the captives, And the opening of the prison to those who are bound;

2 To proclaim the acceptable year of the Lord, And the day of vengeance of our God; To comfort all who mourn,

3 To console those who mourn in Zion, To give them beauty for ashes, The oil of joy for mourning, The garment of praise for the spirit of heaviness; That they may be called trees of righteousness, The planting of the Lord, that He may be glorified.

John 14:16 And I will pray the Father, and He will give you another Helper, that He may abide with you forever—

17 the Spirit of truth, whom the world cannot receive, because it neither sees Him nor knows Him; but you know Him, for He dwells with you and will be in you.

25 These things I have spoken to you while being present with you.

26 But the Helper, the Holy Spirit, whom the Father will send in My name, He will teach you all things, and bring to your remembrance all things that I said to you.

15:26 But when the Helper comes, whom I shall send to you from the Father, the Spirit of truth who proceeds from the Father, He will testify of Me.

16:5 But now I go away to Him who sent Me, and none of you asks Me, "Where are You going?"

6 But because I have said these things to you, sorrow has filled your heart.

7 Nevertheless I tell you the truth. It is to your advantage that I go away; for if I do not go away, the Helper will not come to you; but if I depart, I will send Him to you.

8 And when He has come, He will convict the world of sin, and of righteousness, and of judgment:

9 of sin, because they do not believe in Me;

10 of righteousness, because I go to My Father and you see Me no more;

11 of judgment, because the ruler of this world is judged.

12 I still have many things to say to you, but you cannot bear them now.

13 However, when He, the Spirit of truth, has come, He will guide you into all truth; for He will not speak on His own authority, but whatever He hears He will speak; and He will tell you things to come.

14 He will glorify Me, for He will take of what is Mine and declare it to you.

15 All things that the Father has are Mine. Therefore I said that He will take of Mine and declare it to you.

1 Corinthians 6:19 Or do you not know that your body is the temple of the Holy Spirit who is in you, whom you have from God, and you are not your own?

The printed Scriptures show how God is at work in the world. First, Isaiah 61 is a prophecy of the Messiah, Jesus, and how the Holy Spirit worked in His life to effect our redemption. But it also shows that the Holy Spirit works to anoint preaching and ministries of care, comfort, and liberty to the oppressed.

Second, John 14, 15, 16 are Jesus' own revelation of the work of the Spirit. The Godhead worked together as the Father and the Son prepared for the Spirit to come and be our Helper (Comforter). The Comforter refers to the Spirit standing alongside us and giving us the assurance that God loves us.

The Spirit, present as the Spirit of truth, works to convict us of sin. We cannot be saved by our own decision. The Holy Spirit reveals to us the truth of our condition as sinners. The Spirit shows us the righteousness of God as revealed in Jesus. The Spirit's work is good news to us in that our sinful condition has a remedy: the blood of Christ.

The Spirit deals with Satan on our behalf. Satan, who seeks to judge and condemn us, is himself judged and has no claim upon us as we stand redeemed in Christ.

Third, 1 Corinthians 6:19 shows that the Holy Spirit lives in our own spirits. Our body is the temple of God, the dwelling place on earth of the Holy Spirit. This is why Christians lead holy, moral lives. We are not holy in order to be better than others; we are holy because the Holy Spirit lives within us and we repudiate conscious acts of sinful rebellion against Him.

Global Outreach Emphasis

The Holy Spirit leads sinners to saving faith in Jesus Christ. A person cannot be saved except the Holy Spirit convicts of sin and reveals Christ's righteous provision of mercy and grace through the cross. Thus, when a person accepts Christ as Savior, the Holy Spirit comes to live in the heart. The Spirit's purpose is to be the "guarantee of our inheritance" in Christ (Ephesians 1:14). Justified by faith in Christ, the Holy Spirit pours the Father's love into our hearts (Romans 5:5).

The Holy Spirit continues to work in us through releasing His gifts in our lives (1 Corinthians 6:11; 12:4-7; Romans 12:3-8). Every Christian is given spiritual gifts by the Holy Spirit, and these gifts are to be discovered, developed, and deployed for the cause of Christ. The baptism of the Holy Spirit is for every Christian as an infilling of divine power in our lives to accomplish the ministries that Christ has given us for His glory and for the edification of the church.

Evangelism is the heart-tug of the Holy Spirit. He is at work stirring the hearts of sinners through our faithful witnessing to Christ in words, actions, and attitudes. This is why we should live humbly and faithfully before others. The Holy Spirit uses us in His divine work of preparing them to receive the truth of the gospel.

Word Power
HOLY SPIRIT THEOLOGY AND THE GREAT SCHISM OF 1054

While the Bible is clear in affirming the relationship of the Spirit to the Father and the Son, there were those in early Christianity, and today, who do not recognize the Spirit's deity. The **Faith Declaration** in this lesson contains language reflecting nearly 2000 years of church doctrine relating to the Holy Spirit.

Christian orthodoxy concerning the Trinity was established at Nicaea (325 A.D.), and concerning Christology at Ephesus (431) and Chalcedon (451). The council at Constantinople in 381 rejected the teachings of the *pneumatomachi* (people who were considered "enemies of the Spirit" because they taught that the Holy Spirit was a created being like the angels) and affirmed the deity of the Spirit with the clause found in the Nicene Creed which speaks of the Holy Spirit as "the Lord and Giver of Life, who proceedeth from the Father; who with the Father and the Son together is worshiped and glorified."

Church leaders in the Western church (Rome), including Augustine, saw that the Bible supported the claim that the Holy Spirit was sent by both the Father and the Son (our **Faith Declaration** stands in the context of Western church theology). However, over the centuries, the Eastern church (Greek; Constantinople) disagreed and argued that only the Father sent the Spirit. They objected to the so-called *filioque* clause, "from the Son," of the Creed and considered it an unfaithful addition by the Western church. The Eastern church believed that only the Father sent the Holy Spirit.

The reasons are many and complex, but one of the reasons for the Great Schism of 1054 was this unresolved theological controversy. For a thousand years, Christianity has been divided over this issue between the theologies of the Western church (Roman Catholic, the churches of the Reformation, most Pentecostals) and the theology of the Eastern church (often called the Orthodox churches, including the Greek and Russian Orthodox churches).

ENDNOTES

1. Joseph A. Synan, 1961. Doctrinal amplification of the *Manual of the International Pentecostal Holiness Church, 1993-1997,* LifeSprings Resources, Franklin Springs, Georgia, p. 38. Scriptural texts supporting Synan's statement are John 14:16, 17, 26; 15:26; 16:7-11, 13-15. Synan's statement also shows that there is no difference between the terms "Holy Ghost" and "Holy Spirit." Hebrew (*ruach*) and Greek (*pneuma*) are the same words used interchangeably in the KJV as "Ghost" or "Spirit." There is no distinction between the two as if there were a personal or ministry difference in the Third Person of the Trinity based on the two words. Most contemporary translations recognize this and properly use only the term "Holy Spirit."

2. R. A. Torrey, *The Person and Work of the Holy Spirit*, Zondervan Publishing House, Grand Rapids, Michigan, 1910; 4th printing, 1971, p. 41.

Lesson 4

The Holy Scriptures

Faith Declaration

We believe in the verbal and plenary inspiration of the Holy Scriptures, known as the Bible, composed of sixty-six books and divided into two departments, Old and New Testaments. We believe the Bible is the Word of God, the full and complete revelation of the plan and history of redemption.

Bible Focus

"All Scripture is given by inspiration of God, and is profitable for doctrine, for reproof, for correction, for instruction in righteousness." —2 Timothy 3:16

Lesson Objective

To realize that the Bible is God's Word and determine to live by its teachings.

Global Outreach Emphasis

The Bible reveals God's plan of salvation and the Christian's responsibility to share the good news.

What's This Lesson About?

As children we sang those little songs filled with great truth: "The B-I-B-L-E, yes that's the book for me. I stand alone by the Word of God, the B-I-B-L-E"; and "Jesus loves me this I know, for the Bible tells me so…" Whether in childhood songs or adult longings for spiritual truth, the Bible speaks to us.

Many adults think the Bible is difficult to understand. But when we learn it is God's Word expressed in the history, poetry, and prophecies of Israel; the gospel accounts of Jesus Christ; and the letters of Paul, Peter, and John to churches in Turkey, Greece, and Italy, we discover keys that help us comprehend the wonderful truths revealed in it.

This lesson helps you understand that the Bible is God's own revelation of His plans for humanity. The Holy Spirit used more than forty writers and the span of nearly 1600 years to compose the sixty-six books that Christians believe to be inspired. Those books, from Genesis to Revelation, are the source of our true knowledge of God, Jesus Christ, sin, salvation, the church, and God's purposes for humanity.

1. Inspired
(2 Timothy 3:16, 17)

2 Timothy 3:16 All Scripture is given by inspiration of God, and is profitable for doctrine, for reproof, for correction, for instruction in righteousness,

17 that the man of God may be complete, thoroughly equipped for every good work.

We believe that the Bible is the inspired Word of God; that is, God Himself breathed the words of the Bible to the various writers. It does not mean that God bypassed the writers' mental capacities or the writers were in an ecstatic trance while writing. Rather, they were human instruments through whose thoughts, experience, and language God sent His Word.

This inspiration is verbal and plenary. *Verbal* because every word of the Bible is inspired; *plenary* because every portion of the Bible is inspired. Applied to the original Hebrew, Aramaic, and Greek manuscripts, we can confidently trust the translated versions that have been passed down through the church.[1]

Tragically, the Bible as inspired by God and authoritative in life is rejected and ridiculed by the world. Critics consider the Bible as a religious book with no greater value than any other religious book. The idea that God could and can speak to humanity is rejected on philosophical grounds. This devaluation of the Bible leaves the world in a moral vacuum without knowledge of God.

However, Christians maintain that the Bible is the authoritative Word of God and that God can and does speak to us though it. The Bible gives objective, revealed truth of God. To accept this is to appreciate the reality of interaction between divine and human reason. It is not unreasonable or fanciful to accept the Bible as the Word of God.[2]

John Wesley underscored the truth of God's Word when he wrote, "In the year 1729, I began not only to read, but to study, the Bible as the one, the only standard of truth, and the only model of pure religion."[3] Fifteen years later Wesley, in a Preface to a published collection of forty-four sermons, wrote, "I want to know one thing – the way to heaven; how to land safe on that happy shore. God Himself has condescended to teach the way; for this very end He came from heaven. He hath written it down in a book. *O give me that book! At any price, give me the book of God!* I have it: here is knowledge enough for me."[4]

Wesley's cry is the heart's cry of every Christian, "O give me that book! At any price, give me the book of God!" 2 Timothy 3:16 reveals why we need the Bible. It is God's Word, the sword of the Spirit (Hebrews 4:12), addressing us in truth, reproving and correcting us in the sins and mistakes of life, and instructing us in righteous living. It is the instrument the Holy Spirit uses to make us "complete, thoroughly equipped for every good work" (2 Timothy 3:17).

As the inspired Word of God, the Bible has a four-fold task in making believers complete and equipped for the work of Christ. 2 Timothy 3:16 says the Bible is "profitable," that is, a divine assistance in shaping the life and character of a Christian.

First, the Christian life is shaped by *doctrine*. The Bible provides the content of a Christian's belief system. In biblical thought, doctrine is more than intellectual knowledge. It is knowledge that transforms the way we think and act.

Second, the Christian life is shaped by *reproof*. Gordon Fee writes that this task of the ministry of the Word is to expose and correct false teachers and teachings.[5] The greatest defense against false teachings is to know the whole counsel of God revealed in the Bible.

Third, the Christian life is shaped by *correction*. This is the only time this NT Greek word is used in the Bible. It literally means "to restore to an upright, or right, condition." It relates to the behavioral and ethical life of the Christian. The Bible informs us of the way a Christian should live in this world so as to bring glory to God.

Finally, the Christian life is shaped by *instruction in righteousness*. Paul's use of "instruction" reflects the language of parents teaching a child within the context of family discipline. This is not discipline in the sense of punishment but in the sense of the discipline, focus, energy, and direction that is needful for a full education.

2. Two Testaments
(2 Peter 1:19-21)

2 Peter 1:19 And so we have the prophetic word confirmed, which you do well to heed as a light that shines in a dark place, until the day dawns and the morning star rises in your hearts;

20 knowing this first, that no prophecy of Scripture is of any private interpretation,

21 for prophecy never came by the will of man, but holy men of God spoke as they were moved by the Holy Spirit.

Christians, like Jews, are people of the Book. The Jewish Scriptures, called the Old Testament by Christians, are the Word of God and an indispensable part of the Christian faith. The word *testament* means "covenant." The thirty-nine books of the Old Testament are about the "old covenant" God had with Israel—the covenant revealed to Abraham, Moses, and David.

The twenty-seven books of the New Testament are about the "new covenant" God has with all humanity, in which the promises of God to and through Abraham, Moses, and David are fulfilled in Jesus Christ.

We must remember the Scriptures called the Old Testament are fully the Word of God. We cannot understand the Gospel without them. The Christian church has rightfully resisted every effort to diminish the importance of these Scriptures. In the mid-second century Marcion rejected the Old Testament as the message of an inferior god. The church rightfully rejected this Gnostic heresy. This is one of two errors we must avoid.

The other error is to add another revelation to the Scriptures. This is the error of Mormonism. Christians must be careful that contemporary "prophecies" not take the place of God's revelation in the Bible.

3. Story of Redemption
(John 5:39; 6:63, 68)

John 5:39 You search the Scriptures, for in them you think you have eternal life; and these are they which testify of Me.

6:63 It is the Spirit who gives life; the flesh profits nothing. The words that I speak to you are spirit, and they are life.

68 But Simon Peter answered Him, "Lord, to whom shall we go? You have the words of eternal life."

"Why should I read the Bible? It's just a collection of tales, myths, and out-of-date information that I don't understand anyway," lamented the young, frustrated student. When the student confessed that he didn't understand the Bible, he spoke truthfully. He misunderstood the Bible by thinking it was an ancient philosophy book or an easy-step manual for successful living.

The Bible is God's revelation of His plan of salvation for lost humanity. It is primarily about God's preparation for the Messiah through Israel, the revelation of the Messiah in the person and work of Jesus of Nazareth, and the future when this same Messiah, Jesus, will return to complete the story of redemption.

Examining the Bible, we see how the whole witness of God's Word points to salvation in Jesus Christ:

1. **The Law**[6]—Genesis, Exodus, Leviticus, Numbers, Deuteronomy: God's purposes in creation; humanity's fall into sin; God's plan to save by faith expressed through the life of Abraham; the descendants of Abraham made Egyptian slaves; divine deliverance through Moses; Passover foreshadows the atoning death of Jesus; sacrificial system in the tabernacle prefigures God's dealing with sin through the blood of Christ; Abraham's descendants are the nation, Israel; God's purposes for Israel clearly expressed.

2. **History**—Joshua, Judges, Ruth, 1 and 2 Samuel, 1 and 2 Kings, 1 and 2 Chronicles, Ezra, Nehemiah, Esther: Using broad historical strokes (Joshua, Judges, Samuel, Kings, Chronicles), Israel's history from a loose confederacy of tribes

to a nation under King David, its loss of nationhood after the destruction of Jerusalem in 586 B.C., and God's grace in bringing the captives back from Babylon to Judea, are described. Using more personal touches (Ruth, Ezra, Nehemiah, Esther), Israel's history is told through the lives of these servants of the Lord.

    3. **The Writings**—Job, Psalms, Proverbs, Ecclesiastes, Song of Solomon: The hopes, dreams, pain, suffering, worship, songs, wisdom, and love of humanity for God are expressed in these wonderful expressions of Hebrew poetry. The Psalms are the prayer book of Jesus Christ, including prophecies of His ministry and death.

    4. **The Prophets**—Isaiah, Jeremiah, Lamentations, Ezekiel, Daniel, Hosea, Joel, Amos, Obadiah, Jonah, Micah, Nahum, Habakkuk, Zephaniah, Haggai, Zechariah, Malachi: The history recorded in the historical books is evidenced by the prophetic voice of "thus saith the Lord." The prophetic witness covers a span of 400 years from Joel (about 835 B.C.) to Malachi (about 450 B.C.). The prophets addressed injustice, idolatry, Messiah's first coming in Bethlehem, and Messiah's second coming as the triumphant Son of Man.

    5. **The Gospels**—Matthew, Mark, Luke, John: The church quickly recognized that these "biographies" of Jesus were accurate and inspired accounts of Jesus' earthly ministry. Matthew, Mark, and John were eyewitnesses. Luke wrote his record based on the traditions of the words and deeds of Jesus, which were common knowledge through apostolic preaching and teaching. Through these four books, we learn of the Father's great love for us in sending His Son to die for our sins.

    6. **History**—Acts: New Testament history is living history. The book of Acts is still being written in our lives as the Holy Spirit reveals Jesus and empowers us to serve Him in our generation.

7. **The Letters**—Romans, 1 and 2 Corinthians, Galatians, Ephesians, Philippians, Colossians, 1 and 2 Thessalonians, 1 and 2 Timothy, Titus, Philemon, Hebrews, James, 1 and 2 Peter, 1, 2, and 3 John, Jude: The Holy Spirit has preserved twenty-one letters spanning 40 years across the Mediterranean world. They are practical letters answering the question, "How do we live as Christians?"

8. **Prophecy**—Revelation: Nearly 2000 years ago, the apostle John was given insight into the supremacy of Jesus Christ over this world. This "revelation" of Jesus Christ is not a horror story at the end of the Good News; it is the Good News that Jesus Christ, the Lamb of God, will conquer evil, and God's kingdom will come in fullness as this world shall be redeemed.

Global Outreach Emphasis

The Bible reveals God's plan of salvation and the Christian's responsibility to share the good news. The Bible is the revelation of Good News. Francis Schaeffer wrote that "the Bible gives us true knowledge although not exhaustive knowledge. What the Bible tells us is propositional, factual and true truth, but what is given is in relation to men. It is a scientific textbook in the sense that where it touches the cosmos it is true, propositionally true. The Bible is not a scientific textbook, if by that one means that its purpose is to give us exhaustive truth or that scientific fact is its central theme and purpose."[7]

Applying this to events described in the Bible, Schaeffer added, "When God says, 'Let it be this way,' we can have confidence that this is true history, but that does not mean that the situation is exhaustively revealed or that all our questions are answered. What we know can be true and normative, and yet not be a completely detailed map concerning all the knowledge which God Himself has."[8]

Word Power
NON-CANONICAL WORKS

Some versions of the Bible contain books that Protestants do not consider to be inspired by the Holy Spirit. These books fall into several different categories and are useful for research. Some are useful for devotional reading. However, the church has not granted these books the same status as Scripture for several reasons, including lack of evidence of apostolic authorship and the nature of the material itself. These categories include:

1. **The Apocrypha**—These books were found in the Septuagint (symbol, LXX, Greek translation of the Hebrew Bible) or the Old Latin translation and were accepted by some Jews and Christians as inspired. However, they are not found in the Hebrew Old Testament. These works include Tobit, Judith, The Wisdom of Solomon, Ecclesiasticus, Baruch, the Letter of Jeremiah, the Prayer of Azariah and the Song of the Three Young Men, the History of Susanna, Bel and the Dragon, 1 and 2 Maccabees, 1, 2, 3 Esdras, and the Prayer of Manasseh.

2. **The Apocryphal New Testament**—Dating from the second through sixth centuries of the Christian era, these books include the Arabic Gospel of the Infancy, Assumption of the Virgin, Gospel of Bartholomew, Gospel of the Ebionites, Gospel According to the Hebrews, Gospel of Marcion, Gospel of Thomas.

3. **Pseudepigrapha**—This term describes ancient Jewish writings whose authorship is unknown and which are not considered part of the Bible. These include The Life of Adam and Eve, Ethiopic Enoch, The Testament of the Twelve Patriarchs, The Apocalypse of Baruch, and the Testament of Job.

The Bible is a closed collection of divinely inspired writings. This means that no other books have been or will be written with the same inspiration and authority as these sixty-six books.

ENDNOTES

1. Christians should take time to read a history of the transmission of the Bible over the past 2000 years. While there are minor textual changes due to copyist errors and the like, it is more than evident that the Holy Spirit has faithfully preserved the texts of both the Old and New Testaments through scribes and scholars of the church. Whether reading the *King James Version*, the *New English Bible*, the *New International Version*, the *New King James Version*, or almost any other version, the reader can have confidence that the Word of God has been preserved and faithfully transmitted. There are also paraphrases, such as *The Living Bible* and *The Promise*, which also faithfully convey the message of the Word of God into more contemporary idioms. Christian bookstores have books by evangelical writers that will help you better understand the wonderful history of the transmission of the Bible through the ages.

2. See Ronald H. Nash, *The Word of God and the Mind of Man*, Zondervan, Grand Rapids, Michigan, 1982. See also B. E. Underwood, *The Spirit's Sword—God's Infallible Book*, Advocate Press, Franklin Springs, Georgia, 1969, and Carl F. H. Henry, *Revelation and the Bible*, The Tyndale Press, London, 1958. A more recent book is Josh McDowell's *A Ready Defense*, Thomas Nelson Publisher, Nashville, 1993, especially pages 23-184. McDowell's book is useful for young adults struggling over the authority of the Bible.

3. Rev. John Wesley, *Plain Account of Christian Perfection*, Way of Faith Publishing House edition, Columbia, South Carolina, 1899, p. 4.

4. Rev. John Wesley, *Sermons On Several Occasions*, London, The Epworth Press, 1746, p. vi. italics supplied.

5. Gordon Fee, *1 and 2 Timothy, Titus* in the *New International Biblical Commentary*, Hendrickson Publishers, Peabody, Mass. 1988, p. 280.

6. Often these books are called the Torah. This is more than "law"; it is the revelation of the divine will.

7. Francis A. Schaeffer, "Genesis in Space and Time," *A Christian View of the Bible as Truth*, Volume 2 in *The Complete Works of Francis A. Schaeffer*, Crossway Books, Westchester, Illinois, 1982, pp. 23, 24.

8. Ibid.

Lesson 5

Human Destiny

Faith Declaration

We believe that eternal life with God in heaven is a portion of the reward of the finally righteous; and that everlasting banishment from the presence of the Lord and unending torture in hell are the wages of the persistently wicked.

Bible Focus

"He who believes in the Son has everlasting life; and he who does not believe the Son shall not see life, but the wrath of God abides on him." —John 3:36

Lesson Objective

To acknowledge that heaven and hell are real and accept everlasting life with Christ.

Global Outreach Emphasis

The church must inform the world of the reality of heaven and hell and God's plan of salvation.

What's This Lesson About?

Humanity longs to have some assurance and knowledge of what happens after death. As Ecclesiastes 3:11 reminds us, God has put eternity in the heart of man. Outside the Bible, we know little of human destiny and are left to speculation and delusions from Satan.

But in the Christian faith, we have true knowledge about eternal destiny. John Cooper writes, "From earliest times

Christians have affirmed continuing personal existence after biological death. Members of the early church believed that when the body dies, persons do not completely cease to exist, even temporarily. Rather, they survive in some form or other to enjoy the blessing of God or to suffer his judgment."[1]

There are many questions regarding the great mysteries of divine foreknowledge, election, and human choice. While the Bible does not answer all these questions, it does inform us that God has not created some people predestined for heaven and others predestined for hell without regard to personal choice and accountability. God's will is that all be saved through faith in Christ. The mysteries of divine election and human choice will be revealed in eternity. While those mysteries are yet to be unveiled, the Bible is very clear regarding the only two options available to humanity: those who accept Christ by faith will live eternally in heaven; those who reject Christ will live in everlasting damnation.

1. Heaven
(John 14:1-6)

John 14:1 Let not your heart be troubled; you believe in God, believe also in Me.

2 In My Father's house are many mansions; if it were not so, I would have told you. I go to prepare a place for you.

3 And if I go and prepare a place for you, I will come again and receive you to Myself; that where I am, there you may be also.

4 And where I go you know, and the way you know.

5 Thomas said to Him, "Lord, we do not know where You are going, and how can we know the way?"

6 Jesus said to him, "I am the way, the truth, and the life. No one comes to the Father except through Me."

"As sad as this grave is, I am comforted in knowing that my loved one knew Christ as personal Savior and is with Him. I don't know how sinners can stand it without that knowledge," is something many of us have said and heard. Knowing that a deceased loved one believed in Christ as Savior brings comfort to family and friends. We are encouraged by this truth confirmed in Scripture that in Christ we shall again see that person. Our assurance is based on what Jesus told us, "if I go and prepare a place for you, I will come again and receive you to Myself; that where I am, there you may be also" (John 14:3).

Heaven is both a state of being and a place of spiritual existence. We stare into the expanse of space and wonder where heaven is. It is not part of this created universe. But it is a real place in another dimension of reality. The Bible actually gives more insight into the nature of heaven rather than its location. Millard Erickson observes that "the distinguishing mark of heaven will not be a particular location, but a condition of blessedness, sinlessness, joy, and peace. Life in heaven, accordingly, will be more real than our present existence."[2]

The Bible reveals the following aspects of the nature of heaven. Foremost, heaven is the presence of God (Revelation 21:3). Being in God's presence means there is perfect knowledge (1 Corinthians 13:9-12; 1 John 3:2). Evil and sorrow have no place there (Revelation 21:4). Heaven is a place of great glory (Luke 2:14; Matthew 25:31; Revelation 21:23).

The Bible gives but a glimpse into our life in heaven. This is because the glory of heaven is beyond the capacity of human language (2 Corinthians 12:2-4). But we know that heaven is a place of rest (Hebrews 3:11, 18; 4:9-11). This rest is not inactivity but rather fulfillment of a desired goal and activity without earthbound restraints. Heaven includes worship of God (Revelation 19:1-4). Heaven also involves aspects of continued growth and service (Matthew 19:28; Luke 22:28-30). Finally, heaven is a place of community and fellowship (Hebrews 12:22-24).[3]

2. Hell
(Luke 16:19-31)

Luke 16:19 There was a certain rich man who was clothed in purple and fine linen and fared sumptuously every day.

20 But there was a certain beggar named Lazarus, full of sores, who was laid at his gate,

21 desiring to be fed with the crumbs which fell from the rich man's table. Moreover the dogs came and licked his sores.

22 So it was that the beggar died, and was carried by the angels to Abraham's bosom. The rich man also died and was buried.

23 And being in torments in Hades, he lifted up his eyes and saw Abraham afar off, and Lazarus in his bosom.

24 Then he cried and said, "Father Abraham, have mercy on me, and send Lazarus that he may dip the tip of his finger in water and cool my tongue; for I am tormented in this flame."

25 But Abraham said, "Son, remember that in your lifetime you received your good things, and likewise Lazarus evil things; but now he is comforted and you are tormented.

26 And besides all this, between us and you there is a great gulf fixed, so that those who want to pass from here to you cannot, nor can those from there pass to us."

27 Then he said, "I beg you therefore, father, that you would send him to my father's house,

28 for I have five brothers, that he may testify to them, lest they also come to this place of torment."

29 Abraham said to him, "They have Moses and the prophets; let them hear them."

30 And he said, "No, father Abraham; but if one goes to them from the dead, they will repent."

31 But he said to him, "If they do not hear Moses and the prophets, neither will they be persuaded though one rise from the dead."

Jesus used this story of the rich man and Lazarus as a window into eternity. Prior to the resurrection of Christ, all souls went to either the upper or lower chamber of Hades.[4] The upper portion, called Abraham's bosom, was the abode of the righteous. The lower portion, the abode of the wicked, was known as Hades. On the cross, Jesus told the penitent thief that he would abide that day with Him in Paradise. In His victory over death, Christ led the Old Testament saints out of Abraham's bosom and into heaven while the wicked remain in Hades until the final judgment.

Luke 16 shows us the destiny of those who die in their sins. First, sinners remain conscious and are aware of their suffering. Second, they are tormented in flames of judgment. Third, sinners are not able to depart from this place of judgment and cannot be relieved of their suffering. Fourth, sinners are aware they are punished because of their sins and do not wish for others, still alive on earth, to come to this terrible place of judgment.

But the greatest punishment of the wicked is eternal separation from God and His love. C. S. Lewis describes it as man throughout his life saying to God, "Go away and leave me alone." Hell is God's final response to unrepentant man, "You may have your wish."[5] Hell has no rehabilitation program, no hope of pardon or parole, only the unending reality that a person rejected God's loving offer of salvation.

3. Divine Invitation
(John 3:36)

John 3:36 He who believes in the Son has everlasting life; and he who does not believe the Son shall not see life, but the wrath of God abides on him.

Every person born into this world is a sinner.[6] We cannot save ourselves, and our own good works are but filthy rags when compared to saving grace. There is no way to escape hell except the way provided by Jesus Christ. That is the divine invitation of the gospel—God has done something we cannot do for ourselves: escape hell.

The divine invitation is based on two eternal realities. The first is that the blood of Jesus is the only way that sins are covered and removed from the sight of God. The second is that each person must make a personal decision regarding the truth of the gospel. To reject Christ as Savior is more than rejecting a religious opinion. It is a conscious decision to remain in the righteous wrath of God against sin. It is sinful man's contemptible demand for God to hold him in contempt. It is not God's desire but the sinner's rejection of the Gospel that sends him or her to hell.

Global Outreach Emphasis

The church must inform the world of the reality of heaven and hell and God's plan of salvation. While we cannot control what another person will do, we must not be afraid to tell the truth regarding eternal destiny.

One Saturday morning I joined a group of other Christians at a shopping mall in one-to-one witnessing. I saw an elderly man in his pick-up truck with the door open. He was obviously waiting for someone to return from shopping as well as receiving some of the cooler breeze. I stopped and began small talk looking for an opportunity to share the gospel. As the conversation progressed, I began to talk to him about Christ. When I asked him if he knew he would go to heaven when he died he replied, "Nope." When I asked him if I could tell him about the Lord Jesus Christ, he said he did not care. He was so nonchalant it startled me. I soon realized that he neither knew the Lord nor cared to know Him.

"Sir, do you realize that if you die without Christ you are lost eternally?" I asked.

He replied, "Yes."

In spite of all my efforts, this man, hearing the truth of heaven and hell, had no desire to secure his destiny through the grace of God.

Our responsibility is not to convert people; the Holy Spirit does that. But it is our responsibility to go where people are, find open doors of conversation and friendship, and tell the truth of the saving grace of Jesus Christ.

Word Power
THE JUDGMENT

There will be a final judgment for all people. The righteous will be judged by the Lord and receive their eternal reward (Revelation 20:4, 6). This judgment is called the first resurrection and is a blessing for those who are part of this resurrection. It will be a time of rewards and revelation of how God viewed our efforts for Him on earth (2 Corinthians 5:9, 10; 1 Corinthians 3:11-15).

The last judgment is called the Great White Throne Judgment (Revelation 20:11-15). It is reserved for the wicked of all human history. They will be cast into the lake of fire forever. The lake of fire is also called Gehenna and is a place of everlasting fire (Matthew 5:22; 10:28; James 3:6). Gehenna refers to the valley of Hinnon near Jerusalem which was a trash pile burning continually. Jesus used that name to describe the reality of eternal death and hell.

Another word for hell, *Tartaros*, is used in 2 Peter 2:4 as the place where fallen angels are confined until being cast into the lake of fire.

The apostle Paul implies in Philippians 2:9, 10 that all humanity, including those eternally damned in hell, will acknowledge that Jesus Christ is Lord, to the glory of God. This will not be a confession unto salvation for the lost but will be a confession of truth vindicating the righteous judgment of God. In other words, even the lost will acknowledge that God is just in the punishment they have brought upon themselves by rejecting divine truth and love.

ENDNOTES

1. John W. Cooper, *Body, Soul, and Life Everlasting: Biblical Anthropology and Monism-Dualism Debate*, Williams B. Eerdmans Publishing Company, Grand Rapids, Michigan, 1989, p. 7.

2. Millard J. Erickson, *Christian Theology*, Baker Book House, Grand Rapids, Michigan, 1985, p. 1232.

3. Ibid., pp. 1228-1234.

4. *Hades* is the Greek name for what is called in Hebrew, *Sheol*. In the Old Testament, Sheol is the disembodied state of all who have died, whether good or bad (1 Samuel 28:19).

5. From *The Problem of Pain* and quoted by Erickson, p. 1240. Erickson adds this insightful sentence, "It is God's leaving man to himself, as man has chosen."

6. Many evangelicals and Pentecostals believe that infants, children, and those born with severe mental deficiencies, unable to know the reality of personal sin and the truth of the gospel, are covered by the mercy and grace of God through the sacrificial death of Jesus.

Lesson 6

The Meaning of Salvation

Faith Declaration

We believe that Jesus Christ shed His blood for the remission of sins that are past, for the regeneration of penitent sinners, and for salvation from sin and from sinning.

Bible Focus

"For God so loved the world that He gave His only begotten Son, that whoever believes in Him should not perish but have everlasting life." —John 3:16

Lesson Objective

To know that salvation includes all that God has done for us in Christ and respond to Him with faith and praise.

Global Outreach Emphasis

Jesus Christ died for the sins of the whole world.

What's This Lesson About?

The word *salvation* is often used in the sense of an altar call, "Do you want to be saved?" That use tends to limit salvation simply to our initial response to the gospel. Salvation is a comprehensive term describing the totality of God's redeeming and restoring work in behalf of fallen and lost humanity: the convicting work of the Holy Spirit, the penitent cry of a sinner, the application of the blood of Christ, the reality of justification by faith, sanctifying grace, the baptism of the Holy Spirit, the hope of the resurrection, and a multitude of other graces the Lord gives us. The remaining lessons in this study will focus on different parts of these realities found in the term *salvation*.

The Hebrew verb *to save* has the root meaning of "spaciousness, abundance."[1] Salvation is God's work in our behalf that brings us out of the restricted, closed, and narrow confines of sin and death and into the glorious light, liberty, and gracious presence of His love and life.

1. Forgiveness of Sins
(Matthew 26:28; Ephesians 1:7; Colossians 1:14; 1 John 2:2)

Matthew 26:28 For this is My blood of the new covenant, which is shed for many for the remission of sins.

Ephesians 1:7 In Him we have redemption through His blood, the forgiveness of sins, according to the riches of His grace.

Colossians 1:14 in whom we have redemption through His blood, the forgiveness of sins.

1 John 2:2 And He Himself is the propitiation for our sins, and not for ours only but also for the whole world.

Why do we need forgiveness from God? Because we are guilty of sin against Him. Romans 3:23 informs us that "all have sinned and fall short of the glory of God." Our guilt before God is more than our own awareness of personal guilt; it is true, objective guilt because in heart, mind, and body we are rebellious and seek our own prideful way. But forgiveness is more than an exchange of words. Because of the nature of God's holiness and the nature of sin, divine love must pay the price that meets the demands of holiness and the horrors of sin. That price is the blood of Christ.

Forgiveness of sins is a divine reality based on the blood of Jesus. He is the substitutionary sacrifice for our sins. Because of the perfect sacrifice of Jesus, we have assurance that as "we confess our sins, He is faithful and just to forgive us our sins…" (1 John 1:9). When we call upon the blood of Christ to cover our sins, God remembers our sins no more (Psalm 103:12; Isaiah 43:25). Because God keeps His word, we can resist Satan's accusations against us.

Because blood has been shed to pay the price of our forgiveness, the word *remission* is used in the Faith Declaration above. It is a stronger word than *forgiveness* because it conveys a fuller dimension of what Christ's blood has accomplished for us. As W. E. Vine wrote, "Remission is based upon the vicarious and propitiatory sacrifice of Christ."[2] Noel Brooks adds to this that remission of sins "is release or discharge from our debt of sin, cancellation of its guilt and condemnation, and deliverance from its fearful penalty."[3]

2. Born Again
(Ephesians 2:1-10; John 3:3-8;
2 Corinthians 5:17)

Ephesians 2:1 And you He made alive, who were dead in trespasses and sins,

2 in which you once walked according to the course of this world, according to the prince of the power of the air, the spirit who now works in the sons of disobedience,

3 among whom also we all once conducted ourselves in the lusts of our flesh, fulfilling the desires of the flesh and of the mind, and were by nature children of wrath, just as the others.

4 But God, who is rich in mercy, because of His great love with which He loved us,

5 even when we were dead in trespasses, made us alive together with Christ (by grace you have been saved),

6 and raised us up together, and made us sit together in the heavenly places in Christ Jesus.

7 that in the ages to come He might show the exceeding riches of His grace in His kindness toward us in Christ Jesus.

8 For by grace you have been saved through faith, and that not of yourselves; it is the gift of God,

9 not of works, lest anyone should boast.

10 For we are His workmanship, created in Christ Jesus for good works, which God prepared beforehand that we should walk in them.

John 3:3 Jesus answered and said to him, "Most assuredly, I say to you, unless one is born again, he cannot see the kingdom of God."

4 Nicodemus said to Him, "How can a man be born when he is old? Can he enter a second time into his mother's womb and be born?"

5 Jesus answered, "Most assuredly, I say to you, unless one is born of water and the Spirit, he cannot enter the kingdom of God.

6 "That which is born of the flesh is flesh, and that which is born of the Spirit is spirit.

7 "Do not marvel that I said to you, 'You must be born again.'

8 "The wind blows where it wishes, and you hear the sound of it, but cannot tell where it comes from and where it goes. So is everyone who is born of the Spirit."

2 Corinthians 5:17 Therefore, if anyone is in Christ, he is a new creature; old things have passed away; behold, all things have become new.

The human response to the gospel is conversion, the sinner confessing his or her personal sin(s) and accepting Christ as Savior. The divine response to that confession is what is called *being born again*. Also called *regeneration*, this is the inward work of the Holy Spirit applying the blood of Christ and making us new creatures in Him. Ephesians 2:1, 5 shows that we are spiritually dead and incapable of true spiritual life. Because of Adam's sin, our own natural tendencies are toward sin, and we are unable to change this tendency.

Regeneration reverses the effects of Adam's curse. It is "a restoration of human nature to what it originally was intended to be and what it in fact was before sin entered the human race at the time of the fall."[4] As noble as it may be, nothing humanity does can change our sinful condition. Regeneration is the true transformation desperately needed by sinful humanity.

The new birth is a supernatural event wrought by the Holy Spirit in our hearts. A real personal change occurs in the heart and in one's own self-awareness. Many people exclaim after confession of sin, "I feel clean, like I am brand new." This is a reflection of an inward work of the Spirit. This is also the beginning stage of sanctification leading to the fuller manifestation of that work of grace in the believer's life.

3. Deliverance From Sin
(Romans 6:11-16; 1 John 3:7-9)

Romans 6:11 Likewise you also, reckon yourselves to be dead indeed to sin, but alive to God in Christ Jesus our Lord.

12 Therefore do not let sin reign in your mortal body, that you should obey it in its lusts.

13 And do not present your members as instruments of unrighteousness to sin, but present yourselves to God as being alive from the dead, and your members as instruments of righteousness to God.

14 For sin shall not have dominion over you, for you are not under law but under grace.

15 What then? Shall we sin because we are not under law but under grace? Certainly not!

16 Do you not know that to whom you present yourselves slaves to obey, you are that one's slaves whom you obey, whether of sin leading to death, or of obedience leading to righteousness?

1 John 3:7 Little children, let no one deceive you. He who practices righteousness is righteous, just as He is righteous.

8 He who sins is of the devil, for the devil has sinned from the beginning. For this purpose the Son of God was manifested, that He might destroy the works of the devil.

9 Whoever has been born of God does not sin, for His seed remains in him; and he cannot sin, because he has been born of God.

The born-again believer should not continue in the conscious practice of sins. He will make mistakes, have struggles, face temptations, but should not continue in the old ways of unrighteousness. He knows in his heart there is a new way which is the way of life and not condemnation and death.

There is true deliverance from sin, and it begins with regeneration. The Holy Spirit continues the work of bringing the born-again person into maturity in Christ. The Spirit's work includes inner conviction, the power of prayer, the truth of God's Word, relationships with godly people, and the ministry of the church.

Global Outreach Emphasis

Jesus Christ died for the sins of the whole world. Salvation is for every person. The power of the blood of Christ to forgive sins, renew in His moral image, and deliver from sin is the greatest message of hope the world has ever heard. But unless Christians go and send those who are called to go, the world will remain in spiritual darkness and sin.

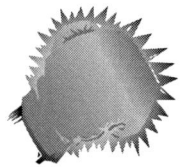

Word Power
OBJECTIVE AND SUBJECTIVE ASPECTS OF SALVATION

To understand the reality of salvation, it is important to distinguish between the objective and subjective aspects of salvation. The objective aspect refers to the spiritual realities that have been established by the atoning work of Christ on the cross. It includes the reality of our changed status before God. Outside Christ, we are sinners under the wrath of God. Through faith in Christ, God views us differently because of what Christ has done for us.

The objective side of salvation, with the accompanying change of status, includes forgiveness of sins, justification, and adoption. These three aspects of initial salvation are all instantaneous and complete through the atoning work of Christ. In God's view, when we confess our sins and accept Christ, we are instantly forgiven of all sins past and present, we are fully justified and declared "not guilty," and we are adopted as sons and daughters of God.

The subjective dimension of salvation refers to the work of the Holy Spirit in applying those objective realities to our personal walk with God. It is the work of the Spirit in bringing a true change in our being, our state, as we are in Christ. This subjective work includes regeneration, sanctification, and glorification.

Regeneration (being born again) is an inward reality of newness of life we personally experience through faith in Christ and the work of the Holy Spirit in us. Regeneration leads to sanctification, in which the believer usually has a definite point of dedication and consecration continuing through life. Finally, our walk with Christ includes movement from glory to glory (2 Corinthians 3:18) in this life as well as the glory of heaven and the glory of the resurrected body (1 Corinthians 15:35-49).

The reality of salvation touches the totality of God's redeeming work for us (objective) and in us (subjective). Thus, we can rejoice in the knowledge that by grace we have been saved, we are being saved, and we shall be saved. This is why forgiveness is based on faith, not feelings. A person may struggle to feel forgiven emotionally or psychologically because he or she is unable to forget specific sins. The power of the gospel is that it is not based on our feelings but on what God has done for us in Christ Jesus. This is why faith, based upon the Word of God, is our only security and hope. The reality of divine forgiveness does not depend upon my emotional struggles; it totally depends upon what God has done. This kind of "saving faith" is the foundation for ultimate spiritual healing and maturity.

ENDNOTES

1. Francis Brown, S. R. Driver, Charles A. Briggs, *A Hebrew and English Lexicon of the Old Testament*, The Clarendon Press, Oxford, England, 1968 edition, p. 446.

2. W. E. Vine, *Expository Dictionary of New Testament Words*, Vol. 2, p. 122. Cited in *The Pentecostal Holiness Advocate*.

3. Noel Brooks, "What Does It Mean To Be Saved?" *The International Pentecostal Holiness Advocate* (Feb. 26, 1978), p. 14.

4. Millard J. Erickson, *Christian Theology*, Baker Book House, Grand Rapids, Michigan, 1985, p. 944.

Lesson 7

Justified by Faith

Faith Declaration
We believe, teach and firmly maintain the scriptural doctrine of justification by faith alone.

Bible Focus
"Having been justified by faith, we have peace with God through our Lord Jesus Christ." —Romans 5:1

Lesson Objective
To acknowledge that we are declared righteous only through faith in Christ and rejoice in His provision.

Global Outreach Emphasis
Sinners find peace with God only through faith in Jesus Christ.

What's This Lesson About?
How can a person stand in the presence of a holy and righteous God? Those who consciously violate God's moral law cannot stand in His presence because of their sin. Those who live moral lives still cannot present themselves pure because of inherited sin from Adam's fall. Thus, the good and the bad are guilty of sin before God.

What can we do? The answer is, "We can do nothing."

What can God do? The answer is, "God can do, and has done, everything necessary for us to stand before Him."

This is justification: God's action to place all our guilt upon Jesus Christ and thereby declare us "not guilty." This is the Good News: God has made in Jesus Christ the way, the only way, for people to stand before Him in peace, joy, and love.

1. Declared Righteous in Christ
(Romans 4:13-25)

Romans 4:13 For the promise that he would be the heir of the world was not to Abraham or to his seed through the law, but through the righteousness of faith.

14 For if those who are of the law are heirs, faith is made void and the promise made of no effect,

15 because the law brings about wrath; for where there is no law there is no transgression.

16 Therefore it is of faith that it might be according to grace, so that the promise might be sure to all the seed, not only to those who are of the law, but also to those who are of the faith of Abraham, who is the father of us all

17 (as it is written, "*I have made you a father of many nations*") in the presence of Him whom he believed, God, who gives life to the dead and calls these things which do not exist as though they did;

18 who, contrary to hope, in hope believed, so that he became the father of many nations, according to what was spoken, *"So shall your descendants be."*

19 And not being weak in faith, he did not consider his own body, already dead (since he was about a hundred years old), and the deadness of Sarah's womb.

20 He did not waver at the promise of God through unbelief, but was strengthened in faith, giving glory to God,
21 and being fully convinced that what He had promised, He was also able to perform.
22 And therefore *"it was accounted to him for righteousness."*
23 Now it was not written for his sake alone that it was imputed to him,
24 but also for us. It shall be imputed to us who believe in Him who raised up Jesus our Lord from the dead,
25 who was delivered up because of our offenses, and was raised because of our justification.

Justified by God means that God pronounces us righteous. We are acquitted, forgiven of our sins by God's action in our behalf. The beauty of the gospel is that God does this while we are unrighteous (Romans 4:5). There is no possible way for us to make ourselves good enough for God. God does for us what we cannot do for ourselves.

J. Rodman Williams describes the "double aspect of God's declaratory righteousness."[1] The first is forgiveness of sins, or non-imputation of sins. Based on Psalm 32:2, cited in Romans 4:8, we have the assurance that God will not count our sins against us as we have faith in Jesus Christ. Because of Jesus Christ, God does not accuse nor condemn us of our sins (Romans 8:33, 34).

The second aspect is the imputation of the righteousness of Jesus Christ. Because Christ has been made sin for us (2 Corinthians 5:21), God has imputed, or counted, our sins as being taken by Christ rather than counting them against us (2 Corinthians 5:19). Since Christ has taken our sins upon Himself, Christ has also given to us His righteousness (2 Corinthians 5:21). This act of pure grace imputes the gift of Christ's righteousness to us, enabling us to stand in the presence of the Father. When God looks at us, He no longer sees us as sinners deserving condemnation, but He sees us covered by the righteousness of Christ.

Some Christians struggle with this wonderful news. We are aware of our sinful thoughts, intentions, and actions. We want to "do" something to prove ourselves worthy of God's grace. But we cannot "do" anything. The very wanting to do something to merit grace is a manifestation of our sinful pride and unbelief in God's free gift.

Yet, God graciously forgives us and counts us righteous in Christ. God loves us so much that He does this independently of our recognition of it. It is a fact established in heaven and secured by the blood of Christ.

2. Received by Faith
(Romans 5:1-11)

Romans 5:1 Therefore, having been justified by faith, we have peace with God through our Lord Jesus Christ,

2 through whom also we have access by faith into this grace in which we stand, and rejoice in hope of the glory of God.

3 And not only that, but we also glory in tribulations, knowing that tribulation produces perseverance;

4 and perseverance, character; and character, hope.

5 Now hope does not disappoint, because the love of God has been poured out in our hearts by the Holy Spirit who was given to us.

6 For when we were still without strength, in due time Christ died for the ungodly.

7 For scarcely for a righteous man will one die: yet perhaps for a good man someone would even dare to die.

8 But God demonstrates His own love toward us, in that while we were still sinners, Christ died for us.

9 Much more then, having now been justified by His blood, we shall be saved from wrath through Him.

10 For if when we were enemies we were reconciled to God through the death of His Son, much more, having been reconciled, we shall be saved by His life.

11 And not only that, but we also rejoice in God through our Lord Jesus Christ, through whom we have now received the reconciliation.

If justification is completely God's work in Christ for us, what can we do to participate in that work? We can do nothing in terms of merit; rather, the only thing we can do is believe in what Jesus has done for us. With tremendous insight, Martin Luther added the word *alone* to the German translation of Romans 3:28, "Therefore we conclude that a man is justified by faith *alone* apart from the deeds or the law." This single word, *alone*, is the capstone of our heritage in Reformation theology.[2]

Saving faith is not blind faith, nor some form of worked up faith, nor faith in faith. Saving faith has a historical object in the atoning death of Jesus Christ. It is faith in what Christ has accomplished for us. Christ has taken the wrath of God, our judgment, upon Himself in our stead. Christ's blood has covered our sin. Christ's righteousness is our righteousness by faith.

If the death of Christ provided atonement for all humanity, why is our personal faith necessary? Our personal faith is God's way of appropriating the benefits of Christ's atonement to us. God can count us as righteous only as we have responded by faith to what Christ has done. Our faith expresses our trust and confidence that God is faithful and just in all He has done.

But this faith is not blind or purely emotional faith. The Reformers (Calvin, Luther, Zwingli) realized that biblical faith has three components: knowledge, assent, and heart-response.[3]

Knowledge means that justifying faith has a true object. This means that saving faith is not merely sincere. You may be sincere but believe in the wrong thing. In justifying faith we have the knowledge that Christ is our righteousness and God declares us not guilty on the basis of who Christ is and what He has done for us. We do not have to know everything or be theological scholars for this faith to be effective. But we must know that our faith is in Christ Jesus. Thus, justifying faith has true content.

Assent refers to intellectual assent; that is, the "assurance or conviction that a certain proposition is true."[4] Related to knowledge, assent is the conviction that the Gospel is true and that it is true *for me*. It is the basis of confidence and assurance that God's Word is true and I can trust the atoning death of Jesus to be sufficient *for me*.

Heart-response is the trusting response of the emotions and will to what God has done for us in Christ.[5] It is a response of gratitude in knowing what God has truly done for us in Christ.

Usually a newborn Christian is not consciously aware of these things happening. It is the role of Christian discipleship to help a new convert come to a better knowledge of what has spiritually happened at conversion. The new babe in Christ is thus fed the meat of the Word of God, enabling growth and maturity in knowledge, commitment, and trust.

3. Purpose of Good Works
(James 2:14-26)

James 2:14 What does it profit, my brethren, if someone says he has faith but does not have works? Can faith save him?
15 If a brother or sister is naked and destitute of daily food,

16 and one of you says to them, "Depart in peace, be warmed and filled," but you do not give them the things which are needed for the body, what does it profit?

17 Thus also faith by itself, if it does not have works, is dead.

18 But someone will say, "You have faith, and I have works." Show me your faith without your works, and I will show you my faith by my works.

19 You believe that there is one God. You do well. Even the demons believe—and tremble!

20 But do you want to know, O foolish man, that faith without works is dead?

21 Was not Abraham our father justified by works when he offered Isaac his son on the altar?

22 Do you see that faith was working together with his works, and by works faith was made perfect?

23 And the Scripture was fulfilled which says, *"Abraham believed God, and it was accounted to him for righteousness."* And he was called the friend of God.

24 You see then that a man is justified by works, and not by faith only.

Jesus said, "Let your light so shine before men, that they may see your **good works** and glorify your Father in heaven" (Matthew 5:16), and "Many **good works** I have shown you from my Father" (John 10:32). The apostle Peter preached that Jesus of Nazareth "went about **doing good**" (Acts 10:38). Obviously there is a proper place and purpose for **good works**.

Ephesians 2:8-10 provides the context from which James 2 is properly understood. First, Ephesians 2:8, 9 reminds us that "by grace you have been saved through faith, and that not of yourselves; it is the gift of God, not works, lest anyone should boast." Thus, this grace concretely manifested in the blessings of justification and appropriated by faith is the ground of our works.

Second, Ephesians 2:10 shows that "we are His workmanship, created in Christ Jesus for good works, which God prepared beforehand that we should walk in them." The good works are specific manifestations of God's love that God has created us to live unto. These good works flow from a justified and redeemed life. It is grace that puts us in the position of truly living for God's purposes in our lives. Good works do not precede justification as a form of merit, but follow justification as evidence of God's transforming grace.

This is the context for James 2:14-26. This apostle resisted a view of Christian life that separated saving faith from changed living. James admonishes us to understand that we are justified by faith so that we can enter into the good works the Father has prepared for us. James' reference to Abraham's willingness to sacrifice Isaac (James 2:21: Genesis 22:1-19) is presented as the evidence that Abraham had truly been justified, counted righteous by God, when he believed the promise of God in Genesis 15:6. Thus, James rightfully shows the relationship of faith and the works that follow as a consequence of our relationship with God. It is important to note that the relationship is not works and faith, but faith leading to good works.

Global Outreach Emphasis

Sinners find peace with God only through faith in Jesus Christ. Sinners seek peace for inner well being, for sanity, for relationships, seemingly in every place except the one place true peace is found. True peace is not found in drugs (whether legal or illegal), nor any person (regardless of commitment and duration of love). The search for true peace must conclude at the cross of Christ or not be concluded at all.

At the cross, sinners discover God's all-forgiving love. The cross bears witness to the fact that the Son of God willingly paid the price for our peace by covering our sins with His blood. This is the

Good News entrusted to us as Christians to share with those who will only find peace as they hear and respond to the gospel.

Word Power
MARTIN LUTHER (1483-1546)

On October 31, 1517, a 34-year-old theology instructor at Wittenberg, Germany, wrote a letter to the Archbishop of Mainz that included 95 theses, or points of disputation. The young instructor posted these 95 theses in Latin on the Castle Church doors in Wittenberg that very day. This young doctor of theology, a Catholic priest in the Order of Augustinian Hermits, started a revolution that changed Christianity and Western culture.

Originally protesting against the sale of indulgences,[6] Luther's letter to Cardinal Albrecht, the Archbishop of Mainz, included these concerns about those who bought indulgences: "The poor souls believe that when they have bought indulgence letters, they are then assured of their salvation... They also believe that man is freed from every penalty and guilt by these indulgences." Luther then added to the Cardinal, "O great God! The souls committed to your care, excellent Father, are then directed to death."[7]

Luther's protest was based on the new understanding of the righteousness of God he found in a series of lectures he prepared on the Psalms, Romans, Galatians, and Hebrews. Years later he wrote about his struggles and study leading up to October 1517. He said that he "hated" the phrase in Romans 1:17, "in it [the gospel of Christ] the righteousness of God is revealed," because all he could see was a "righteous God who punishes sinners"; but the Holy Spirit led him to the truth of the righteousness of God, namely, "that the righteousness of God is that through which the righteous live by a gift of God, namely by faith. Here I felt as if I were entirely born again and had entered paradise itself..."⁸ Because of what Christ has done for us, we receive this gift of grace by faith in Christ. This meant that salvation was by faith "alone."

Luther's theological contributions included a return to Scripture, the Bible, as the sole source of true doctrine, the fact that our salvation is in Christ alone, that salvation is by grace alone, and that we receive salvation by faith alone.

ENDNOTES

1. J. Roman Williams, *Renewal Theology: Salvation, the Holy Spirit, and Christian Living*, Vol. 2, Zondervan Publishing House, Grand Rapids, Michigan, 1990, p. 64ff.

2. Although Luther added the German word *allein* (alone), it is a rightful interpretation of the apostle Paul's meaning in Romans and his other writings. Luther did not "add" to the Word of God; rather, like any good translator, he used appropriate language to express the truth that Paul communicated.

3. R. C. Sproul, *Faith Alone: The Evangelical Doctrine of Justification*, Baker Book House, Grand Rapids, Michigan, 1995, p. 75-88.

4. Ibid., p. 78.

5. Ibid., p. 82ff.

6. Indulgences were statements of forgiveness of sins for oneself and for others in purgatory. They were sold and purchased in order to raise funds for the medieval Catholic Church. Pope Clement IV in 1343 issued a Bull (authoritative church pronouncement) formulating the theory of indulgences and equating them with money. The Black Death in the mid-1300s led to an expansion of this practice. By the time of Luther, indulgences were common practice, and the particular indulgence arousing Luther's ire was the one being used to build St. Peter's in Rome.

7. Jaroslov, Pelikan, ed., *Luther's Works*, Volume 48, Fortress Press, Philadelphia, p. 46.

8. Timothy George, "Luther's Theology," *Christian History*, Volume 34, 1995.

Lesson 8

Sanctification

Faith Declaration

We believe that Jesus Christ shed His blood for the complete cleansing of the justified believer from all indwelling sin and from its pollution, subsequent to regeneration.

We believe in sanctification. While sanctification is initiated in regeneration and consummated in glorification, we believe that it includes a definite, instantaneous work of grace achieved by faith subsequent to regeneration. Sanctification delivers from the power and dominion of sin. It is followed by lifelong growth in grace and knowledge of our Lord and Savior Jesus Christ.[1]

Bible Focus

As He who called you is holy, you also be holy in all your conduct, because it is written, *"Be holy, for I am holy."*
—1 Peter 1:15, 16

Lesson Objective

To discover that Christ's sacrifice made possible Christian purity and maturity and live victoriously in Him.

Global Outreach Emphasis

A godly life is a witness to the world of God's power to deliver from sin's bondage.

What's This Lesson About?

When a sinner accepts Jesus Christ as Savior, two important spiritual effects are justification and regeneration. Though justification describes our standing before God as being declared righteous through faith in Christ, inward sanctification begins "in the moment a man is justified."[2]

Regeneration is the new birth, made a new creature in Christ, whereby there is a real change in our personal condition. Regeneration "marks the beginning point of sanctification" in terms of self-awareness of God's work in us. This means that "we have been given that power over sin which is the birthright of every child of God as we seek to be conformed to His image."[3]

Rooted solidly in Scripture, rediscovered in the 18th century by John Wesley, and shaped by 19th-century American revivalism, the holiness churches have shown how sanctifying grace transforms the redeemed person and changes ethical behavior.

1. Christ, Our Sanctifier
(1 John 1:7-9)

1 John 1:7 But if we walk in the light as He is in the light, we have fellowship with one another, and the blood of Jesus Christ His Son cleanses us from all sin.

8 If we say that we have no sin, we deceive ourselves, and the truth is not in us.

9 If we confess our sins, He is faithful and just to forgive us our sins and to cleanse us from all unrighteousness.

Jesus Christ is made unto us sanctification (1 Corinthians 1:30). Jesus prayed to the Father in our behalf that we be sanctified by divine truth (John 17:17, 19). Hebrews 2:11 affirms that "He who sanctifies and those who are being sanctified are all of one…" 2 Thessalonians 2:13 encourages us with the knowledge that "God from the beginning chose you for salvation through sanctification by the Spirit and belief in the truth." Hebrews 10:14 assures us that "by one offering He has perfected forever those who are being sanctified."

The confession that Christ is our sanctifier means three things: 1) His victory at the cross includes sanctifying power over the dominion of sin; 2) His sanctifying work is the will of the Father and the activity of the Holy Spirit in our lives; 3) Sanctification is a divine work of grace in our behalf which we receive by faith.

We do not receive sanctification by works nor earn it by good behavior. Sanctification is a gift of grace which we receive by faith. Our cooperation is in relationship to the disciplines of the Christian life which are made alive to us by the Holy Spirit.

2. Cleansed From Indwelling Sin
(Romans 6:1-11)

Romans 6:1 What shall we say then? Shall we continue in sin that grace may abound?

2 Certainly not! How shall we who died to sin live any longer in it?

3 Or do you not know that as many of us as were baptized into Christ Jesus were baptized into His death?

4 Therefore we were buried with Him through baptism into death, that just as Christ was raised from the dead by the glory of the Father, even so we also should walk in newness of life.

5 For if we have been united together in the likeness of His death, certainly we also shall be in the likeness of His resurrection,

6 knowing this, that our old man was crucified with Him, that the body of sin might be done away with, that we should no longer be slaves of sin.

7 For he who has died has been freed from sin.

8 Now if we died with Christ, we believe that we shall also live with Him,

9 knowing that Christ, having been raised from the dead, dies no more. Death no longer has dominion over Him.

10 For the death that He died, He died to sin once for all; but the life that He lives, He lives to God.

11 Likewise you also, reckon yourselves to be dead indeed to sin, but alive to God in Christ Jesus our Lord.

Although our sins are forgiven when we accept Christ as Savior, there remains our sinful nature and condition inherited from Adam's fall. Sometimes called the old man, the carnal nature, or the Adamic nature, it is that part of the moral image of God that was lost in the fall. This condition leads us to live according to the flesh.[4] Wesley understood that sanctification meant "to be renewed in the image of God, in righteousness and true holiness."[5]

This sinful nature is identified in Ephesians 4:22, 25-31 and Colossians 3:5-11. These passages describe the character of persons born again but enslaved by indwelling sin. Such persons are controlled by "deceitful lusts" (4:22) which are manifested in lying, out-of-control anger, giving the devil place and opportunity in life, stealing, grieving the Holy Spirit, living with bitterness, wrath, clamor, and evil speaking. Colossians 3 further reveals the condition of Christians struggling with and dominated by fornication, passion, evil desire, covetousness, malice, filthy language, and deception.

How are we cleansed from these things which Satan uses to destroy our witness and our joy, and which ultimately can cost us our salvation? How are we renewed in the image of God?

There is only one answer: the blood of Jesus Christ. In Psalm 51, King David asks the Lord to forgive him of personal sin (adultery, murder: cf. 2 Samuel 11, 12) and to sanctify his sinful nature: "I was brought forth in iniquity, and in sin my mother conceived me. Behold, You desire truth in the inward parts…Purge me with hyssop, and I shall be clean; Wash me, and I shall be whiter than snow. Create in me a clean heart, O God…" (vv. 5-7, 10).

We are sanctified and renewed by recognizing that by accepting the benefits of Christ we have died to sin.[6] We are to "reckon" (consider) ourselves dead to sin and alive to God in Christ (Romans 6:11). We grow in grace through prayer, Christian fellowship, worship, and knowledge of the Bible. The Holy Spirit uses the Word of God to expose our sinful selves, apply the blood of Christ, and continually renew us in the image of Christ.

Are we ever completely free from the dominion of indwelling sin? Wesley answered, "Undoubtedly, or how else can we be said to be saved from our uncleanness? (Ezekiel 36:29)."[7] The Bible confirms God's power to cleanse from indwelling sin through the sanctifying blood of Christ (2 Corinthians 7:2; 1 John 1:7, 9).

3. Victory Over Sin
(Romans 6:15-23)

Romans 6:15 What then? Shall we sin because we are not under law but under grace? Certainly not!

16 Do you not know that to whom you present yourselves slaves to obey, you are that one's slaves whom you obey, whether of sin leading to death, or of obedience leading to righteousness?

17 But God be thanked that though you were slaves of sin, yet you obeyed from the heart that form of doctrine to which you were delivered.

18 And having been set free from sin, you became slaves of righteousness.

19 I speak in human terms because of the weakness of your flesh. For just as you presented your members as slaves of uncleanness, and of lawlessness leading to more lawlessness, so now present your members as slaves of righteousness for holiness.

20 For when you were slaves of sin, you were free in regard to righteousness.

21 What fruit did you have then in the things of which you are now ashamed? For the end of those things is death.

22 But now having been set free from sin, and having become slaves of God, you have your fruit to holiness, and the end, everlasting life.

23 For the wages of sin is death, but the gift of God is eternal life in Christ Jesus our Lord.

In the previous section, we looked at the cleansing of the sin nature. This cleansing purifies our hearts from the dominion of sin and frees us from the overriding desire to sin. It turns our hearts toward loving God and others in truth and righteousness. Although we pray each day to be forgiven of our sins (Matthew 6:12), we do so with confidence because we have an Advocate with the Father, Jesus Christ (1 John 2:1).

Many Christians live defeated because they fail to distinguish between sinful guilt before God and the limitations inherent in human existence. Wesley considered such limitations to include imperfect knowledge, ignorance, mistakes in judgment and actions, weakness and slowness of understanding, and temptations.[8]

In particular, Satan attacks new converts and the newly sanctified with the idea that the awareness of temptation is in itself a sin against God. 1 Corinthians 10:13 and James 1:12-15 clearly show that awareness of temptation is not the same as moral guilt before God. Christ was tempted yet was without sin (Matthew 4:1-11; Hebrews 2:18; 4:15, 16). The same is true for us as we come to Christ in our temptations and find His grace is sufficient to keep us from falling (Jude 24).

There is a second aspect of our victory over sin. We are set apart for the glory of God in our relationships and service to Him. God can more fully and fruitfully use a sanctified life for His glory. Freedom from the dominion of sin leads us to freedom as servants of Christ. The purpose of being sanctified and delivered from sin's bondage is to release us to greater love of God, fruitfulness in the Spirit, and fulfillment of God's eternal purpose for us.

Global Outreach Emphasis

A godly life is a witness to the world of God's power to deliver from sin's bondage. Wesley rightly understood that holiness enables us to love the Lord with all our hearts and our neighbors as ourselves. Holiness is not about imposing rules upon ourselves or others but is about loving people in the truth and spirit of Christ. It is this love, pure and rooted in the love of God, that enables us to put aside our own wills and do the will of Christ.

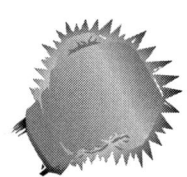

Word Power
CLARIFICATIONS OF SANCTIFICATION

Sometimes we misunderstand certain aspects of the doctrine of holiness (sanctification). Holiness is not about a legalistic code. It is about renewal in the image of Christ and love of God and neighbor. This implies lifestyle changes reflecting that transformation but always in an attitude of humility and service and not judgment upon others.

Sanctification is not greater than justification or regeneration. It is the spiritually natural outgrowth of being redeemed by the blood of Christ and belonging to Him.

Complete cleansing from indwelling sin and its pollution subsequent to regeneration refers to "taking away the sin principle."[9] This is sometimes called the "negative side of sanctification" (that is, in the sense that something is removed, rendered ineffective); or "the circumcision of the heart so as to make it possible for us to love the Lord our God with all our heart and soul" (Acts 26:18; Ephesians 5:25-27; Titus 2:14; Hebrews 9:13, 14; 10:10, 14-22; 13:11, 12; Galatians 2:20; Romans 8:5-10).[10] The fact that it is *subsequent to regeneration* means that it is growth, crisis, and continued growth following our new birth in Christ. The defeat of the sin nature through the cross of Christ frees us from the dominion, or lordship, of sin and enables us to love and serve God with our whole hearts. It does not free us from temptations to sin, human weaknesses of intellect, emotions, and psychological stresses. But sanctification provides true victory over sin through the course of life.

Definite instantaneous refers to the so-called "crisis" aspect of sanctification. Sanctification, because it includes a "death to the dominion of sin," is a *definite*, real, spiritual experience rooted in the provision of Christ and experienced through the Holy Spirit in our lives. *Instantaneous* refers to the use of the aorist tense in Greek, indicating a completeness, though not a finality, of this work of grace in our lives. These terms together indicate there is a clear "breakthrough" over the dominion of sin for the child of God.[11]

Received by faith refers to the fact that like justification by faith, the baptism of the Holy Spirit, and every spiritual blessing from God, sanctification is received by faith. God honors faith and responds graciously to our trusting in Him for cleansing from sin and consecration of our lives to His will and service.

A review of sanctification as related to the work of salvation is appropriate. In *Scriptural Holiness*, Noel Brooks provides this overview:

(1) The sinner is prepared for the gospel by prevenient grace operating through the Holy Spirit and human circumstances;

(2) The gospel calls us as "the Holy Spirit illuminates the darkened mind of the sinner with divine truth under Christian preaching and teaching";

(3) The Holy Spirit convicts of sin, bringing personal awareness of guilt and condemnation;

(4) The sinner repents and turns away from the life of sin and its guilt;

(5) Repentance and faith merge so that the Holy Spirit creates a loving trust of God;

(6) Faith leads to union with Christ; that is, being "in Christ";

(7) From this union comes justification, whereby the sinner is declared righteous by God because of faith in Christ. This includes personal awareness of forgiveness of sins;

(8) Regeneration follows in that being born again, the redeemed person is given the life of Christ;

(9) Sanctification is the development of the regenerate life and includes growth, crisis victory over the carnal nature, and continued growth in the Lord;

(10) Sanctification reaches its climax and ultimate fulfillment in glorification, when the redeemed person will be reunited with a redeemed, resurrected body at the return of Christ.

This overview does not imply a person is aware of distinct differences between certain theological terms such as repentance, justification, and regeneration. In fact, these happen simultaneously and are divided in the overview for clarification.[12]

ENDNOTES

1. These paragraphs are Articles 9 and 10 of the International Pentecostal Holiness Church. Article 10 was recently adopted as revised (1997) by the church and provides a broader perspective on the church's teaching regarding sanctification. It reflects the Scriptural understanding that regeneration is the starting point of sanctification, leading to the fullness of this experience in this earthly life, and

ultimate completion in heaven. The Articles together affirm that sanctification is not achieved through human effort but is a gift of grace, received by faith, and provided by the cleansing blood of Christ.

2. John Wesley, *A Plain Account of Christian Perfection*, Way of Faith Publishing House, Columbia, SC, 1899, p. 31. Wesley added, "Yet sin remains in him, yea, the seed of all sin, till he is sanctified throughout. From that time (justification) a believer gradually dies to sin, and grows in grace." In keeping with the Protestant understanding of justification, righteousness is not infused into us but rather we are declared righteous by God because of our faith in Christ.

3. Melvin E. Dieter, "The Wesleyan View" in *Five Views On Sanctification*, Zondervan Publishing House, Grand Rapids, 1987, pp. 16, 17.

4. In this sense, the "flesh" denotes those things that seek fulfillment from this passing world. It includes actions, attitudes, and orientation of the self in relation to the world. A person can be morally pure in actions, yet filled with sin in terms of finding fulfillment in this world rather than in God.

5. John Wesley, p. 30.

6. This can be called "positional sanctification" in that it is a spiritual reality based on our relationship to Christ. Because we are "in Christ," we are truly sanctified in Him. Our personal appropriation and application of this spiritual reality continue throughout life as we grow in Christ.

7. John Wesley, p. 31. Wesley drew an important distinction between sin and the imperfections of life. Holiness does not mean sinless perfection. Wesley did not teach such, and we do not believe such. The complete cleansing from inward sin gives us a heart sensitive to, and seeking for, God and His love. We still make mistakes of judgment and misinformation and have other flaws. Sanctification cleanses our heart so that we seek the Lord above all else.

8. Ibid., p. 13, 14.

9. J. A. Synan, "Doctrinal Emphasis," *1993 Manual of the International Pentecostal Holiness Church*, p. 40.

10. Ibid.

11. Noel Brooks, *Scriptural Holiness*, Advocate Press (now LifeSprings Resources), Franklin Springs, GA, 1967, p. 56. This work contains an excellent survey of holiness in the Old and New Testaments and is particularly insightful regarding sanctification as part of the total salvation work of God, and the place and role of the crisis experience in our lives.

12. Ibid., p. 43, 44.

Lesson 9

The Pentecostal Experience

Faith Declaration

We believe that the pentecostal baptism of the Holy Ghost and fire is obtainable by a definite act of appropriating faith on the part of the fully cleansed believer[1], *and the initial evidence of the reception of this experience is speaking with other tongues as the Spirit gives utterance.*

Bible Focus

"The promise is to you and to your children, and to all who are afar off, as many as the Lord our God will call." —Acts 2:39

Lesson Objective

To examine the connection between prophecy regarding the coming of the Holy Spirit and its fulfillment on the Day of Pentecost, and to be filled with the Spirit.

Global Outreach Emphasis

The Holy Spirit empowers Christians to tell the good news of Jesus Christ.

What's This Lesson About?

Besides His work in justification, regeneration, and sanctification, the Holy Spirit is the agent who empowers believers for Christian service.[2] The next lesson will focus on various manifestations of the

Spirit through signs and gifts. This lesson shows you how God's plans for us have been fulfilled in the sending of the Holy Spirit on the Day of Pentecost. You will discover that the Holy Spirit who was at work in the Old Testament is the same Holy Spirit at work in the church today.

1. The Spirit Promised
(Joel 2:28-32)

Joel 2:28 And it shall come to pass afterward That I will pour out My Spirit on all flesh; Your sons and your daughters shall prophesy, Your old men shall dream dreams, Your young men shall see visions.

29 And also on My menservants and on My maidservants I will pour out My Spirit in those days.

30 And I will show wonders in the heavens and in the earth: Blood and fire and pillars of smoke.

31 The sun shall be turned into darkness, And the moon into blood, Before the coming of the great and awesome day of the Lord.

32 And it shall come to pass That whoever calls on the name of the Lord Shall be saved, For in Mount Zion and in Jerusalem there shall be deliverance, As the Lord has said, Among the remnant whom the Lord calls.

Nearly 800 years before the events of Acts 2, the Judean prophet Joel foretold a mighty outpouring of the Holy Spirit. In Joel's day, the prophecy related to a great agricultural calamity by which locusts destroyed the crops. Joel interpreted this as the judgment of God upon disobedient Judah.

The Joel prophecy that was fulfilled on the Day of Pentecost contains three important themes that are significant for the church. The first is that the Spirit is poured out upon all believers with no distinctions in age, gender, or sociological status. "All flesh" that has turned to God will receive this mighty move of God. Thus, the Pentecostal baptism is not simply for a few but for all who will open their hearts to God's mighty presence.

The second aspect is that the Pentecostal experience is related to end-time preparation and judgment; that is, the Day of the Lord. For 2,000 years, the Spirit has been working through the church to prepare the church and the world for the return of Christ.

The third aspect is that the Pentecostal experience is deeply evangelistic. The news of coming judgment is not to condemn the world but to warn sinners to repent and call on the name of the Lord. A Spirit-filled church will be an evangelistic church concerned about its community and the world.

2. Promise Fulfilled
(Acts 2:1-4)

Acts 2:1 When the Day of Pentecost had fully come, they were all with one accord in one place.

2 And suddenly there came a sound from heaven, as of a rushing mighty wind, and it filled the whole house where they were sitting.

3 Then there appeared to them divided tongues, as of fire, and one sat upon each of them.

4 And they were all filled with the Holy Spirit and began to speak with other tongues, as the Spirit gave them utterance.

The Day of Pentecost[3] was an established holy day for Jews. In the Bible, this festival is variously called the Feast of

Weeks (Leviticus 23:15-22; Deuteronomy 16:9-12), the Feast of Harvest (Exodus 23:16; 34:22), or the day of firstfruits (Numbers 28:26-31), and was the spring celebration of the firstfruits of the wheat harvest. It was one of the three Jewish feasts in which males were required to come to Jerusalem. Pentecost followed Passover (which symbolizes salvation from sin) and is associated with the harvest (evangelism).

In Acts 2 we see the convergence of the three themes elucidated in Joel 2. First, the Holy Spirit came upon 120 followers of Jesus. There were men and women, rich and poor, Galileans and Judeans. They had been faithful to obey Christ and were in unity, prayer, and fellowship. Pentecostal power was not just for the twelve male disciples but was for everyone with a loving obedience of Christ.

Second, Peter immediately understood that what they had received was in fulfillment of Joel 2 (Acts 2:16-21). His preaching recognized the judgment of God against sin manifested in the death and resurrection of Christ (2:22-32).

Third, the Holy Spirit enabled Peter and the others to witness to the lost concerning salvation through Christ. This is the first purpose of the gift of tongues. On the day of Pentecost, tongues were given as a way of sharing the gospel with people of other languages. Today, tongues may occasionally function in that way but more often, as the initial evidence, function to give us boldness to share our faith with those whom we meet as the Spirit gives opportunities.

Acts 2 shows that this experience was not psychologically induced by people. First, the sound came "from heaven"; that is, from beyond the group gathered in the upper room. The sound was like "a rushing mighty wind." Jesus taught that the Spirit blows where He wills and is not under the control of people (John 3:8). The people actually saw the presence of the Spirit as tongues of fire which were upon each of them. Fire is a symbol of the Holy Spirit and indicates purity through the presence of God and His voice (Exodus 3:1-5; see **Word Power** for insights on speaking in tongues).

3. The Baptism of the Holy Spirit
(Acts 19:1-6)

Acts 19:1 And it happened, while Apollos was at Corinth, that Paul, having passed through the upper regions, came to Ephesus. And finding some disciples

2 he said to them, "Did you receive the Holy Spirit when you believed?" So they said to him, "We have not so much as heard there is a Holy Spirit."

3 And he said to them, "Into what then were you baptized?" So they said, "Into John's baptism."

4 Then Paul said, "John indeed baptized with a baptism of repentance, saying to the people that they should believe on Him who would come after him, that is, on Christ Jesus."

5 When they heard this, they were baptized in the name of the Lord Jesus.

6 And when Paul had laid hands on them, the Holy Spirit came upon them, and they spoke with tongues and prophesied.

The "Ephesian Pentecost" shows that the Pentecostal experience is a distinct theological and often experiential event in the lives of believers. Paul encountered godly men in Ephesus who were Christians with limited knowledge. They were followers of the baptism of John the Baptist described in Matthew 3:1-12. Jesus submitted to this baptism and began His earthly ministry from that point (Matthew 3:13-17). But there remained disciples of John who spread his message of repentance across the Mediterranean world.

It was such a group that Paul met during this visit to Ephesus. Their conversation led Paul to ask if they had received the Holy Spirit when they believed. This can refer to either: 1) the Holy Spirit living in them at conversion; or 2) the Pentecostal baptism. After teaching the full truth of salvation, Paul baptized these men in the name of the Lord Jesus.[4]

Paul then taught these men concerning the baptism in the Holy Spirit and laid his hands upon them, praying for their personal reception of this experience. The men spoke with tongues and prophesied as signs that they had indeed received the baptism in the Holy Spirit.

Global Outreach Emphasis

The Holy Spirit empowers Christians to tell the good news of Jesus Christ. As we have seen from Joel 2 and Acts 2, the Pentecostal experience has as a primary object the enabling of believers to share the gospel effectively. Added significance comes when we realize that Acts 2 is the divine remedy to the confusion of language and division among peoples expressed in the tower of Babel incident (Genesis 11). In order to save humanity from its own self-destruction, God confused the languages.

But God's redemptive will is to unite humanity under the banner of the cross of Christ. The Holy Spirit gives believers the capacity to tell the saving story of Christ to people of all languages. Even when the Spirit does not give us foreign languages to speak, He nonetheless enables us to speak with words and expressions that people can comprehend.

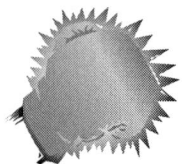

Word Power
GLOSSOLALIA

Pentecostal churches have historically held that glossolalia, or speaking in tongues, is the initial evidence of the baptism in the Holy

Spirit. This view is based on the recorded incidents in Acts where tongues accompanied the presence of the Spirit:

- Acts 2:4: Day of Pentecost, 120 people spoke in other tongues;
- Acts 8:14-19: although tongues are not specifically mentioned, some physical manifestation occurred because Simon saw evidence that when the apostles laid hands on the people, they received the Spirit;
- Acts 9:17: Saul (Paul) was filled with the Holy Spirit; although tongues are not mentioned here, the apostle indicated in 1 Corinthians 14:18 that he spoke in tongues more than any of the Corinithian believers;
- Acts 10:44-47: Gentile believers spoke in tongues when they received the baptism in the Holy Spirit;
- Acts 19:1-6: Ephesian believers spoke in tongues when they received the baptism in the Holy Spirit.
- Acts 2:4 shows the relationship between the Holy Spirit and an individual in speaking in tongues. The Spirit gives the utterance. The Greek word translated "utterance" is also used in 2:14 where Peter preached the first Pentecost sermon and in 26:25 where Paul told Festus, "I am not mad ... but speak (utter) the words of truth and wisdom." The word means "to enunciate clearly, to declare." Thus, the utterance the Spirit gives has an evangelistic leaning and is not gibberish or mumblings. The Spirit gives something distinct to our own minds or spirits, and He expects us to obey His prompting.

We are "to speak" these other tongues which are in our spirit. This is the human cooperation: open one's mouth and speak. The Greek word is the normal word for "speak." It is an act of obedience to cooperate with the inner promptings of the Holy Spirit and declare what He gives us to speak.

This means that when a person receives the baptism of the Holy Spirit, the human will is not bypassed by the Holy Spirit.

He invites us to cooperate in the release of His presence and power in our lives manifested through our obedience in speaking.

How do you receive the baptism of the Holy Spirit? First, know you are saved by the grace of God and receive forgiveness of any known sins in your life. Second, be committed to obey Christ and serve Him with your heart, soul, mind, and body. Third, ask the Holy Spirit, who already lives in you through faith in Christ, to manifest His power, enabling you to serve Christ more effectively. Fourth, as you confess His name and praise Him for His love and blessings, speak whatever He gives you.

ENDNOTES

1. The "fully cleansed believer" is a reference to sanctification. It does not refer to sinless perfection but rather to that attitude of heart committed to live in service and love to God. It implies a life oriented toward obeying God. As we saw in the previous lesson, sanctification has its beginnings in regeneration. A person who has accepted Christ as Savior may in the same moment appropriate victory over sin, love toward God through commitment to service, and receive the baptism in the Holy Spirit with the evidence of tongues. While justification, sanctification, and the baptism in the Spirit are distinct theologically, they are not necessarily distinct in time and personal experience. Although the Faith Declaration uses the phrase "baptism of the Holy Spirit," sometimes writers draw a distinction between the "baptism **of** the Holy Spirit" as referring to the Spirit's work in justification and regeneration and "baptism **in** the Holy Spirit" as referring to the Pentecostal experience.

2. See Lesson 3 for additional information about the Spirit's work in justification, regeneration, and sanctification It is important to remember that the Spirit lives in our hearts when we accept Christ as Savior. When a new convert is baptized in water, he is baptized into Christ (Romans 6:3; Ephesians 4:4-6), and the Spirit is present as the guarantee of our salvation (Ephesians 1:13, 14). The Pentecostal baptism is theologically distinct from water baptism in that it a spiritual baptism in the Spirit with emphasis upon empowerment.

3. Pentecost is the Greek word for *fifty*, indicating the number of days following Passover.

4. This should not be construed to mean that Paul did not baptize using the Trinitarian formula ("in the name of the Father, the Son, and the Holy Spirit"). Rather, it denotes the fact that the spiritual experience of these disciples needed to be completed in the atoning work of Christ and not just repentance of sins associated with John.

Lesson 10

Living in the Spirit

Faith Declaration

We believe that the pentecostal baptism of the Holy Ghost and fire is obtainable by a definite act of appropriating faith on the part of the fully cleansed believer, and the initial evidence of the reception of this experience is speaking with other tongues as the Spirit gives utterance.[1]

Bible Focus

"If we live in the Spirit, let us also walk in the Spirit."
—Galatians 5:25

Lesson Objective

To discover the purpose of spiritual gifts in the church and learn to walk in the Spirit.

Global Outreach Emphasis

The church is effective in ministry as Christians discover, develop, and deploy their spiritual gifts.

What's This Lesson About?

Learn the three **D's: Discover, Develop,** and **Deploy.** That's what it's about when it comes to serving Christ through His Church. Many people who have received the baptism in the Holy Spirit and attend Pentecostal churches thought that living a Spirit-filled life meant only speaking in tongues and living a moral life.

Some people have not understood, nor even been taught, about the ultimate purposes of spiritual gifts in the life of the believer and the community of faith. In this lesson you will **Discover** that the Bible has much to tell us about effective Christian living. This knowledge will help you **Develop** the spiritual gifts you have as a child of God. Finally, in the context of a worshiping, loving, and obedient community of faith, you will find the ministry of being **Deployed** for service in your spiritual gifts.

What? You don't think you have any spiritual gifts? When the Holy Spirit made you alive in Christ, you became the temple of the Holy Spirit (I Corinthians 3:16; 6:19). You're still not sure? Don't worry. As you study this lesson, you will find direction regarding God's plan for you!

1. The Purpose of Tongues
(1 Corinthians 14:1-5)

1 Corinthians 14:1 Pursue love, and desire spiritual gifts, but especially that you may prophesy.

2 For he who speaks in a tongue does not speak to men but to God, for no one understands him; however, in the spirit he speaks mysteries.

3 But he who prophesies speaks edification and exhortation and comfort to men.

4 He who speaks in a tongue edifies himself, but he who prophesies edifies the church.

5 I wish you all spoke in tongues, but even more that you prophesied; for he who prophesies is greater than he who speaks with tongues, unless indeed he interprets, that the church may receive edification.

There are three ways that speaking in tongues is described in the New Testament. The first is the evidence of the baptism in the Holy Spirit (discussed in Lesson 9). The Holy Spirit speaks through us as a personal and public witness of His presence empowering us in our service for Christ.

The second use, the gift of tongues, is described in 1 Corinthians 14. It is the use of tongues as a special manifestation of the Spirit within the context of the community of faith. Such a message should be interpreted and not left unintelligible to the hearers.[2] The reason for this is obvious. If people are constantly speaking in unknown tongues, no one will understand what God is seeking to do. That is why Paul preferred prophecy, that is, speaking God's truth in the language of the listeners, over uncontrolled speaking in tongues. Paul did not reject the use of tongues in the worship service; but he did insist that tongues spoken by an individual should be interpreted or the tongues speaker should keep the message to himself (1 Corinthians 14:27, 28).[3]

The third use is speaking in tongues in personal prayer, praise, and song to the Lord. Paul referred to this in 1 Corinthians 14:15 and indicates that there are appropriate times in the worshiping community and in our own personal lives to pray and sing in unknown tongues. These tongues do not require interpretation because they function for the edification of the speaker or as expressions of Spirit-led intercession (Romans 8:26, 27).[4]

2. Gifts of the Spirit
(Romans 12:6-8, 1 Corinthians 12:27-31; Ephesians 4:11-16)

Romans 12:6 Having then gifts differing according to the grace that is given to us, let us use them: if prophecy, let us prophesy in proportion to our faith;

7 or ministry, let us use it in our ministering; he who teaches, in teaching;

8 he who exhorts, in exhortation; he who gives, with liberality; he who leads, with diligence; he who shows mercy, with cheerfulness.

1 Corinthians 12:27 Now you are the body of Christ, and members individually.

28 And God has appointed these in the church: first apostles, second prophets, third teachers, after that miracles, then gifts of healings, helps, administrations, varieties of tongues.

29 Are all apostles? Are all prophets? Are all teachers? Are all workers of miracles?

30 Do all have gifts of healings? Do all speak with tongues? Do all interpret?

31 But earnestly desire the best gifts. And yet I show you a more excellent way.

Ephesians 4:11 And He Himself gave some to be apostles, some prophets, some evangelists, and some pastors and teachers,

12 for the equipping of the saints for the work of ministry, for the edifying of the body of Christ,

13 till we all come to the unity of the faith and of the knowledge of the Son of God, to a perfect man, to the measure of the stature of the fullness of Christ;

14 that we should no longer be children, tossed to and fro and carried about with every wind of doctrine, by the trickery of men, in the cunning craftiness of deceitful plotting,

15 but, speaking the truth in love, may grow up in all things unto Him who is the head—Christ—

16 from whom the whole body, joined and knit together by what every joint supplies, according to the effective working by which every part does its share, causes growth of the body for the edifying of itself in love.

There are three main ways that spiritual gifts are used in the church.[5] First, Ephesians 4 announces the equipping gifts of apostles, prophets, evangelists, pastor-teachers.[6] These gifts are the foundational leadership gifts of the Christian church. These are people whom God calls and equips for the purpose of equipping His people in the church so they can do the work of ministry. Perhaps this is the greatest contribution of the modern Pentecostal/charismatic movement: the rediscovery that pastors and evangelists (and the other equipping gift offices) are not the ministers of the church, but they equip people to minister in order to edify the body of Christ.

Second, Romans 12 gives the body ministry gifts. Every believer at conversion is given one or more of these gifts. These are the gifts enabling the church to be the church in practical, daily worship of God and service to humanity. They are often related to one's talents and abilities in life.

Third, 1 Corinthians 12, while including some of the equipping gifts, also includes manifestation gifts of tongues, interpretation, healings, etc. While God may use certain individuals more than others in these gifts, these gifts should not glorify the individual but are manifestations of divine majesty, power, and grace.

3. The Fruit of the Spirit
(Galatians 5:22-25)

Galatians 5:22 But the fruit of the Spirit is love, joy, peace, longsuffering, kindness, goodness, faithfulness,

23 gentleness, self-control. Against such there is no law.

24 And those who are Christ's have crucified the flesh with its passions and desires.

25 If we live in the Spirit, let us also walk in the Spirit.

The fruit of the Spirit can be described as the personality of Jesus reflected in human hearts. It is true that we have this treasure in earthen vessels (2 Corinthians 4:7); but transformation of the human heart through the presence of the Holy Spirit is greater than the weaknesses of human flesh. That's why Galatians 5 is about attitudes of the heart reflecting genuine love for God and our neighbor.

The gifts of the Spirit are for building up the body of Christ and making the church more effective in reaching a hurting world. The gifts are not trophies of personal achievement, pride, or self-promotion, nor indications that one Christian is better than another Christian. The fruit of the Spirit provides the personal context of genuine love, patience, hope, and care for one another.

Remember that it is the *fruit* (singular) of the Spirit listed in Galatians 5. These nine fruit are actually dimensions of the one fruit of the life of Jesus in us. This is not a buffet of spiritual goodies from which we pick and chose. As we surrender ourselves to Christ each day, He will bring this fruit to greater maturity in our lives.

Global Outreach Emphasis

The church is effective in ministry as Christians discover, develop, and deploy their spiritual gifts. Spiritual gifts are the tools the Lord gives us as He uses us to further the cause of the Great Commission. Every Christian, at various stages of life, is gifted for the purpose God has ordained for each believer. The active young Christian is gifted to meet the opportunities of his generation. The middle-aged Christian has maturity, experience, and perhaps additional finances that the Spirit uses in the church. The senior adult, perhaps confined to home due to poor health, is still gifted for usefulness to the church through time for concentrated intercessory prayer.

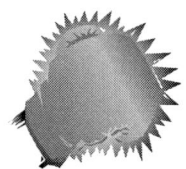

Word Power
THE GREATEST GIFT

1 Corinthians 12 is the apostle Paul's discussion of various spiritual gifts and their relationship to the body of Christ. The apostle left no doubt that gifts are meant to build the church as people serve the cause of Christ together. While some gifts may bring greater visibility, no person is greater than another in relation to God's purposes for us.

1 Corinthians 14 is Paul's discussion of how two specific, more visible gifts, tongues and prophecy, are meant to function in the church. His guidelines are practical and serve to reinforce the principles established in 1 Corinthians 12.

But between those chapters is the Great Love Chapter of the Bible, 1 Corinthians 13. The context could not be more appropriate. Paul's poem to divine love is set within the context of spiritual gifts. Love is the "more excellent way" of the gifts (1 Corinthians 12:31). Love is the greatest gift to be pursued with all eagerness and desire (1 Corinthians 14:1).

Living in the Spirit means to live in the power and presence of Christ's love. All our gifts, sermons, giving, worship, and anything else associated with church are in vain if we have not love. The absence of love negates the righteous and eternal impact of our lives.

There's no doubt that God wants us to *serve* in the power of the *gifts* of the Spirit. But more importantly, God wants us to *live* in the power of His wondrous *love*.

ENDNOTES

1. This Faith Declaration is the same as in Lesson 9. It is repeated here as the basis for further understanding of the Pentecostal experience in the Christian life.

2. The word *interpret* does not mean *translation*. The interpretation may be longer, or shorter, in actual time than the message in tongues. The Spirit gives the interpretation so that people may understand what He is saying to the church at that given time. Unless a human foreign language is spoken and someone in the church who speaks that language can *translate*, most manifestations of tongues are meant to be *interpreted*; that is, the essence, or spirit, of the message is given in the known language of the hearers.

3. It may surprise you to realize that the apostle Paul knew that spiritual gifts, especially manifestation gifts like tongues, should be used wisely in conjunction with human will and order in the church. Paul told the Corinthians that if one of them had a message in tongues, but knew no one was present to interpret, that person should keep it to himself in private prayer. That is not a sign of disobedience; rather, it is a sign of submission to authority and recognizing the place of order in the church.

4. Many commentators believe that Paul is describing speaking in tongues in Romans 8:26, 27. This is the common Pentecostal interpretation. This means that such prayer, while not intelligible to the speaker or any hearer present, is nonetheless prayer in the will of God. It is the Spirit praying through us to the Father and Son in perfect accord.

5. B. E. Underwood, *Spiritual Gifts: Ministries and Manifestations* (Franklin Springs, GA; Advocate Press [now LifeSprings Resources], 1984). While there are many excellent books on the market, Underwood's insights reflect the traditional Pentecostal perspective, provide a readable way of understanding spiritual gifts, and discuss how they operate in the church and individuals. Use this book as an elective study for a class or congregation to discover, develop, and deploy its spiritual gifts.

6. Some commentators separate pastors and teachers into a fourth and fifth equipping gift. The syntax points to pastors and teachers as one primary gift; however, it is not inappropriate to think of Bible teachers and theologians as equipping teachers of the church.

Lesson 11

Divine Healing

Faith Declaration
We believe in divine healing as in the atonement.

Bible Focus
"He was wounded for our transgressions, He was bruised for our iniquities; The chastisement for our peace was upon Him, And by His stripes we are healed." —Isaiah 53:5

Lesson Objective
To acknowledge that Christ provided for our healing in His atonement and to praise Him.

Global Outreach Emphasis
Christians can minister to the needs of a hurting world through the name of Jesus Christ.

What's This Lesson About?
God is concerned about our spiritual, emotional, psychological, and physical health. The Bible repeatedly tells of healing miracles as expressions of God's love for humanity. There are at least a dozen healing miracles in the Old Testament and at least two dozen in the New Testament (e.g., Genesis 20:17, 18; Genesis 21:1, 2; Exodus 15:23-25; Numbers 21:6-9; 1 Kings 13:6; 17:17-24; 2 Kings 2:21, 22; 4:32-37; Mark 1:40-45; 3:1-6; 5:25-34; Luke 13:10-17; 17:11-19; John 5:1-18).

Our need for healing arises from Adam and Eve's sin in Genesis 3. The Fall, and its aftermath of exclusion from the

Garden of Eden, separated humanity from God, one another, and one's self. Original sin has affected the entire created order. The creation yearns for its deliverance "from the bondage of corruption" (Romans 8:19-22) that is part of the universal consequences of Adam's sin. All human sicknesses — including those of genetic, environmental, and psychological causes — and death are ultimately the bitter fruit of Adam's disobedience against God (Romans 5:12-21).

In response to the human predicament, God mercifully intervenes to restore and save. Two extremes must be avoided to maintain a biblical understanding of divine healing. The first extreme is to conclude that God never intervenes miraculously to heal. This is the view of cynics, skeptics, and some theologies that argue that healing concluded with the demise of the first apostles. The second extreme is to conclude that God will physically heal in this life everyone who has faith. Such is the view of proponents of divine health, hyper-faith, and theologies that emphasize the human will at the expense of divine sovereignty.

The texts in this lesson will help us find the biblical balance of prayer, faith, hope, and trust in God's love for us now and for eternity.

1. The Human Need
(Luke 8:43-48; Acts 3:1-10)

Luke 8:43 Now a woman, having a flow of blood for twelve years, who had spent all her livelihood on physicians and could not be healed by any,

44 came from behind and touched the border of His garment. And immediately her flow of blood stopped.

45 And Jesus said, "Who touched Me?" When all denied it, Peter and those with him said, "Master, the multitudes throng and press You, and You say, 'Who touched Me?'"

46 But Jesus said, "Somebody touched Me, for I perceived power going out from Me."

47 Now when the woman saw that she was not hidden, she came trembling; and falling down before Him, she declared to Him in the presence of all the people the reason she had touched Him and how she was healed immediately.

48 And He said to her, "Daughter, be of good cheer; your faith has made you well. Go in peace."

Acts 3:1 Now Peter and John went up together to the temple at the hour of prayer, the ninth hour.

2 And a certain man lame from his mother's womb was carried, whom they laid daily at the gate of the temple which is called Beautiful, to ask alms from those who entered the temple;

3 who, seeing Peter and John about to go into the temple, asked for alms.

4 And fixing his eyes on him, with John, Peter said, "Look at us."

5 So he gave them his attention, expecting to receive something from them.

6 Then Peter said, "Silver and gold I do not have, but what I do have I give you: In the name of Jesus Christ of Nazareth, rise up and walk."

7 And he took him by the right hand and lifted him up, and immediately his feet and ankle bones received strength.

8 So he, leaping up, stood and walked and entered the temple with them — walking, leaping, and praising God.

9 And all the people saw him walking and praising God.

10 Then they knew that it was he who sat begging alms at the Beautiful Gate of the temple; and they were filled with wonder and amazement at what had happened to him.

The incidents from Luke 8 and Acts 3 reveal the following regarding the plight of the human condition:

First, the woman's use of medical treatment is not condemned; rather, the limits of medicine are portrayed. Luke, the writer of Luke and Acts and companion of the apostle Paul, was a physician by training and practice. While medical science does much to improve health and bring recovery from disease and injury, in this woman's case, it had done nothing to help her.

Second, the lame man never dreamed he would be able to walk; he thought of his future solely in terms of financial security. Money was all he expected from anyone who walked near him.

While the human need is desperate, the response of redeeming love is more than sufficient. The woman was healed by divine power that flowed from Christ. He did not heal by psychological suggestion or magic. He healed by the power vested in Him as the Son of God, the redeemer of humanity. Jesus responded personally to her need and recognized her faith in Him.

As Peter and John ministered healing life to the lame man in Acts 3, believers today can intercede and reach to the hurting around us through the name of Jesus Christ. The Lord still heals and seeks willing servants who will trust Him and minister to those in need.

2. Atonement Provides Healing

(Isaiah 53:4, 5; 1 Peter 2:24, 25)

Isaiah 53:4 Surely He has borne our griefs And carried our sorrows; Yet we esteemed Him stricken, Smitten by God, and afflicted.

5 But He was wounded for our transgressions, He was bruised for our iniquities; The chastisement for our peace was upon Him, And by His stripes we are healed.

1 Peter 2:24 who Himself bore our sins in His own body on the tree, that we, having died to sins, might live for righteousness—by whose stripes you were healed.

25 For you were like sheep going astray, but have now returned to the Shepherd and Overseer of your souls.

Healing is part of the redeeming work of Christ, a work in its spiritual dimensions completed in His death on the cross. Through His shed blood, we have forgiveness of sins, are justified by faith in Him, and receive the benefits of holiness as we are sanctified by and through Him. These spiritual benefits are part of our salvation.

Salvation also includes the blessings of healing in this life and the promise of ultimate healing and restoration in heaven and in the resurrection.

That is why we believe that healing is part of the atoning work of Christ in our behalf. This belief is supported by the printed text (also see Matthew 8:16, 17). Christ's healings are not simply acts of compassion; they are signs of His divine power and victory over sin and death. Although He healed prior to His death, the spiritual reality of His healings was and is rooted in the atonement. The atonement is the basis for reconciliation to God and all the blessings flowing from it.

When we pray for healing today, we pray with confidence because we are asking for the victory of Christ on the cross to be applied in our present situation. This is neither fanciful nor wishful thinking; it is true prayer based on the true victory Christ has wrought in our behalf.

3. Faith To Receive Healing
(James 5:13-16)

James 5:13 Is anyone among you suffering? Let him pray. Is anyone cheerful? Let him sing psalms.

14 Is anyone among you sick? Let him call for the elders of the church, and let them pray over him, anointing him with oil in the name of the Lord.

15 And the prayer of faith will save the sick, and the Lord will raise him up. And if he has committed sins, he will be forgiven.

16 Confess your trespasses to one another, and pray for one another, that you may be healed. The effective, fervent prayer of a righteous man avails much.

Faith that heals is not blind faith nor faith in faith, but faith in Jesus Christ. The apostle James places this faith in the context of Christian community and the spiritual benefits of the atonement.

First, James recognizes that sickness is more than a private matter for the Christian. Sick Christians are to call for the elders of the church. The sick have an initiative act in their own healing; this initiative is a sign of faith. The elders respond with two specific actions. They are to pray over the sick person and anoint him with oil in the name of the Lord. Oil is a symbol of the Holy Spirit, and anointing implies touching the sick person. Together, these things constitute the "prayer of faith" that "will save the sick." It is important to note that the word "save" is used here, indicating something more than improvement of the physical condition. Healing is a manifestation of the total work of salvation and includes the spiritual, emotional, and relational condition of the sick person. The result of this prayer of faith is that "the

Lord will raise him up." The specific act of healing is left to the Lord and His intentions for this person.

Second, prayers of healing include reconciliation as provided in the atonement. The sick need to be in genuine Christian fellowship and not isolated from family and friends. Sometimes sickness will cause us to realize there are things not spiritually right in our lives. The sickness becomes the divine opportunity to be reconciled to God, other people, and ourselves as we confess sins the Holy Spirit brings to our awareness. This passage does not teach that sickness is due to personal sin; rather, it teaches that sickness can be used to make us more sensitive to the Holy Spirit and our personal spiritual condition.

Global Outreach Emphasis

Christians can minister to the needs of a hurting world through the name of Jesus Christ. The Christian faith has inspired the greatest advances in medicine and other expressions of benevolence in the world. This is based on the conviction that God cares for the well-being of His creatures.

Care for the poor, the homeless, the hungry, and those shattered by natural calamities, shows the love of Christ for a wounded world. While it may not lead to actual conversions at that moment, such care is part of the Holy Spirit's work in preparing people to receive the love of God through the Gospel.

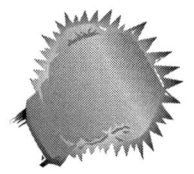

Word Power
ISSUES RELATED TO HEALING:

● *Is there any relationship of personal sin to sickness?* Jesus clearly taught in John 9:3 that not all sickness is due to personal sin. Much sickness is due to the curse resulting from Adam's fall, and we are prone to illness due to environment, genetics, and the like. However, there are instances where personal behavior can cause illness. Smoking leads to cancer; unhealthy eating habits can lead to heart attacks and strokes; immoral sexual behavior can lead to sexually transmitted diseases. We must be careful not to condemn the sick, regardless of circumstances, because we do not know the full story. We are called to comfort, pray, anoint, and be avenues of healing grace to the whole person.

- *Are all people healed who pray with faith?* The answer is no. Does that imply a lack of faith on the part of the person praying? Usually not. Many people go through illness feeling condemned because they are not healed as they expected to be. Our theology of healing must balance encouragement to pray for specific healing with recognition of divine sovereignty in our lives.

- *What about Christians who die from illness?* This does not imply failure by the person or family in prayers or treatment or failure by God. For the Christian, the ultimate healing is heaven and the resurrection. Even in sickness, our primary goal is that God receive glory and His will, if it is not healing in this specific illness, be accomplished as we walk with Him.

- *Will God heal a person who is not a Christian?* The Bible shows that people who were not part of Israel or the church were healed (2 Kings 5; Acts 16:16-19). God loves all people and healings in their behalf are signs of His love giving them opportunity to respond to the Gospel. We should not be hesitant to pray for healing for those who do not know the Lord as Savior but should wisely use this as an opportunity for His power to be manifested.

- *What about the gifts of healings found in 1 Corinthians 12?* It is important to note the plural of this particular gift. It denotes the multiplicity of God's healing grace for the human condition. Every Christian can and should pray for the sick. God does seem to give certain people a special anointing of healing as they pray for the sick. Christians can rejoice that God makes provision for us through the blood of Christ and obey Him in every situation.

Lesson 12

Christ's Second Coming

Faith Declaration

We believe in the imminent, personal, premillennial second coming of our Lord Jesus Christ, and love and wait for His appearing.

Bible Focus

"...Be ready, for the Son of Man is coming at an hour you do not expect." —Matthew 24:44

Lesson Objective

To know that Christ's second advent is at hand and anticipate His return.

Global Outreach Emphasis

Recognizing that Christ will return soon, the church must send workers into the harvest.

What's This Lesson About?

For two thousand years the church has prayed *Maranatha*, "Our Lord, Come" (1 Corinthians 16:22, Aramaic language). In our time, Spirit-filled Christians still offer this prayer, yearning for the return of the Lord Jesus Christ.

The Faith Declaration emphasizes the *imminent* return of Jesus Christ. This means that Christ could return soon. God's time clock of divine intervention of human history is all that matters.

The Declaration also emphasizes the *personal* return of Christ. This means that the Lord Himself will return. We believe that the same Jesus who has coexisted eternally with the Father and the Spirit, the same Jesus who was conceived of the Holy Spirit in the womb of the virgin Mary, the same Jesus who died on the cross and arose the third day, **this** same Jesus will return in power and glory.

Finally, the Declaration emphasizes the *premillennial* second coming of Christ. This means that Christ will return to establish the thousand years of peace of His victorious presence upon the earth.

1. Signs of the Last Days
(Matthew 24:3-14; 2 Thessalonians 2:1-12)

Matthew 24:3 Now as He sat on the Mount of Olives, the disciples came to Him privately, saying, "Tell us, when will these things be? And what will be the sign of Your coming, and of the end of the age?"

4 And Jesus answered and said to them, "Take heed that no one deceives you.

5 "For many will come in My name, saying, 'I am the Christ,' and will deceive many.

6 "And you will hear of wars and rumors of wars. See that you are not troubled; for all these things must come to pass, but the end is not yet.

7 "For nation will rise against nation, and kingdom against kingdom. And there will be famines, pestilences, and earthquakes in various places.

8 "All these things are the beginnings of sorrows.

9 "Then they will deliver you up to tribulation and kill you, and you will be hated by all nations for My name's sake.

10 And then many will be offended, will betray one another, and will hate one another.

11 "Then many false prophets will rise up and deceive many.

12 "And because lawlessness will abound, the love of many will grow cold.

13 "But he who endures to the end shall be saved.

14 "And this gospel of the kingdom will be preached in all the world as a witness to all the nations, and then the end will come."

2 Thessalonians 2:1 Now, brethren, concerning the coming of our Lord Jesus Christ and our gathering together to Him, we ask you,

2 not to be soon shaken in mind or troubled, either by spirit or by word or by letter, as if from us, as though the day of Christ had come.

3 Let no one deceive you by any means; for that Day will not come unless the falling away comes first, and the man of sin is revealed, the son of perdition,

4 who opposes and exalts himself above all that is called God or that is worshiped, so that he sits as God in the temple of God, showing himself that he is God.

5 Do you not remember that when I was still with you I told you these things?

6 And now you know what is restraining, that he may be revealed in his own time.

7 For the mystery of lawlessness is already at work; only He who now restrains will do so until He is taken out of the way.

8 And then the lawless one will be revealed, whom the Lord will consume with the breath of His mouth and destroy with the brightness of His coming.

9 The coming of the lawless one is according to the working of Satan, with all power, signs, and lying wonders,

10 and with all unrighteous deception among those who perish, because they did not receive the love of the truth, that they might be saved.

11 And for this reason God will send them strong delusion, that they should believe the lie,

12 that they all may be condemned who did not believe the truth but had pleasure in unrighteousness.

The last days are characterized by increased international conflict, increased famine, pestilence, and earthquakes, increased spiritual deception, and the appearance of the antichrist. It is widespread spiritual deception and the revelation of the man of sin, the man of perdition, and the overwhelming spirit of lawlessness, that will most characterize the last days. The spirit of lawlessness refers to casting off all moral restraint in every area of human enterprise.

In the last days, organized religion will exist but will be rendered ineffective by moral and intellectual relativism. The antichrist will fill this vacuum and provide the world a person whom it can adore and raise to the stature of God. The world will worship antichrist as he assumes his place of power, signs, and wonders.

The apostle Paul saw that this deception will be successful because people "did not receive the love of the truth" and were more interested in "pleasure in unrighteousness" (2 Thessalonians 2:10, 12).

2. Jesus Christ Will Return
(Matthew 24:27-31; Revelation 19:11-16)

Matthew 24:27 For as the lightning comes from the east and flashes to the west, so also will the coming of the Son of Man be.

28 For wherever the carcass is, there the eagles will be gathered together.

29 Immediately after the tribulation of those days the sun will be darkened, and the moon will not give its light; the stars will fall from heaven, and the powers of the heavens will be shaken.

30 Then the sign of the Son of Man will appear in heaven, and then all the tribes of the earth will mourn, and they will see the Son of Man coming on the clouds of heaven with power and great glory.

31 And He will send His angels with a great sound of a trumpet, and they will gather together His elect from the four winds, from one end of heaven to the other.

Revelation 19:11 Now I saw heaven opened, and behold, a white horse. And He who sat on him was called Faithful and True, and in righteousness He judges and makes war.

12 His eyes were like a flame of fire, and on His head were many crowns. He had a name written that no one knew except Himself.

13 He was clothed with a robe dipped in blood, and His name is called The Word of God.

14 And the armies in heaven, clothed in fine linen, white and clean, followed Him on white horses.

15 Now out of His mouth goes a sharp sword, that with it He should strike the nations. And He Himself will rule them with a rod of iron. He Himself treads the winepress of the fierceness and wrath of Almighty God.

16 And He has on His robe and on His thigh a name written: KING OF KINGS AND LORD OF LORDS.

Christ's return will occur in two stages. The first stage, the rapture, will occur when Christ comes as a thief in the night to remove believers from the impending Great Tribulation (1 Thessalonians 4:15-18; 5:2-4). The second stage will be the return of Christ in power and glory following the Great Tribulation.

When Christ returns in power and glory, He will finalize His victory over Satan. Satan's dominion over the earth will be broken, and a thousand years of peace will be established as Christ reigns. We believe that the millennium will be achieved by the personal presence of Jesus Christ when an angelic being binds Satan for a thousand years.

Christ's return will take place following the Battle of Armageddon, where He defeats the antichrist, the beast, and false prophet who have deceived the world and sought to destroy Israel. By the power of His Word, Christ will destroy all these enemies.

After this battle, there will be a final resurrection of all the righteous, who will receive their rewards at the judgment (Revelation 20:4, 6). Following the millennium, Christ will allow Satan to return to the earth for one final effort of deception. Satan will be crushed for eternity following this defeat (Revelation 20:7-10). Then the final judgment upon all who did not confess Christ will occur at the Great White Throne Judgment (Revelation 20:11-15). After this judgment, the new heaven, new earth, and new Jerusalem will be revealed as the eternal abode of God and the redeemed (Revelation 21, 22).

3. Power for Living
(2 Peter 3:10-14)

2 Peter 3:10 But the day of the Lord will come as a thief in the night, in which the heavens will pass away with a great noise, and the elements will melt with fervent heat; both the earth and the works that are in it will be burned up.

11 Therefore, since all these things will be dissolved, what manner of persons ought you to be in holy conduct and godliness,

12 looking for and hastening the coming of the day of God, because of which the heavens will be dissolved, being on fire, and the elements will melt with fervent heat?

13 Nevertheless we, according to His promise, look for new heavens and a new earth in which righteousness dwells.

14 Therefore, beloved, looking forward to these things, be diligent to be found by Him in peace, without spot and blameless.

There is a divine connection between the return of Christ and God's call for us to be holy. Godly living prepares us personally for the Lord's return and also witnesses to the lost of God's power over sin. The Holy Spirit empowers us in holy conduct and godliness so we can appear before Christ "in peace, without spot and blameless."

Global Outreach Emphasis

Recognizing that Christ will return soon, the church must send workers into the harvest. We live in the eleventh hour (Matthew 20:9) when the Holy Spirit is seeking people of these final generations to serve Him. Although evil abounds in these last days, the power of the Holy Spirit is greater, enabling believers to reach the lost around the world. This is the time for finances, plans, and personal priorities to be poured into world evangelism and reap this harvest of souls before it is too late.

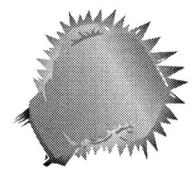

Word Power
THE BOOK OF REVELATION:

Probably no book of the Bible has caused more confusion and uncertainty than the last book of the Bible, the prophecy of John called *The Revelation of Jesus Christ*. It is unfortunate that many Christians are afraid of this book and afraid of Christ's return. The second coming of Christ is a source of great hope, comfort, and encouragement for Christians. We can rightly think of Revelation as a "fifth Gospel." It contains words of the Risen Lord to His church and tells of His plans to redeem the earth, ridding it of Satan's curse and presence.

The main character of Revelation is Jesus Christ. He is revealed as the Lord of heaven and earth, who is worshiped and is worthy of all praise, glory, honor, and dominion. Jesus is the Lamb, slain from the foundation of the world, worthy to receive the title deed of the earth from the Father and open it, thereby releasing redeeming power.

The scroll of Revelation 5:1-7, is God's title deed to earth. Beginning in Revelation 6:1, Christ opens the seals of this scroll, releasing divine judgment upon sin. The things described from Revelation 6-19 are not caused by Satan but are God's plan to fully expose Satan and lead our enemy to the place of final defeat.

Christians can take heart that the book of Revelation is both pastoral and prophetic. It reminds us that God has given His eternal Word that evil will not prevail but will be defeated by righteousness and justice.

Lesson 13

The Meaning and Mission of the Church

Faith Declaration
We believe it is the responsibility of every believer to dedicate his life to carrying out the work of the Great Commission.

Bible Focus
"Go into all the world and preach the gospel to every creature." —Mark 16:15

Lesson Objective
To understand the meaning and purpose of the Church and obey Christ's Great Commission.

Global Outreach Emphasis
The church is Christ's body on earth and is called to fulfill the Great Commission.

What's This Lesson About?
Jesus Christ established the church, and He continues to build it. When a sinner accepts Christ as Savior, he becomes a member of the body of Christ and belongs to the church universal. A born-again believer should become

a member of a local congregation in order to experience the communion of the saints with God and one another.

The study of the church is called ecclesiology. This lesson, the final in this study, is about our role and mission as people who have been called out from the world and called into the fellowship of the Redeemer and the redeemed.

The church is not the brick and wood of the building in which you are meeting. The church is the people who have been born again by the blood of Christ. You are the church. Here is your mission!

1. What Is the Church?
(Matthew 16:18-19; Acts 4:32-35)

Matthew 16:18 And I also say to you that you are Peter, and on this rock I will build My church, and the gates of Hades shall not prevail against it.

19 And I will give you the keys of the kingdom of heaven, and whatever you bind on earth will be bound in heaven, and whatever you loose on earth will be loosed in heaven.

Acts 4:32 Now the multitude of those who believed were of one heart and one soul; neither did anyone say that any of the things he possessed was his own, but they had all things in common.

33 And with great power the apostles gave witness to the resurrection of the Lord Jesus. And great grace was upon them all.

34 Nor was there anyone among them who lacked; for all who were possessors of lands or houses sold them, and brought the proceeds of the things that were sold,

35 and laid them at the apostles' feet; and they distributed to each as anyone had need.

The foundation of the church is the confession that Jesus is the Christ, the Son of the living God (Matthew 16:16). This is the "rock" upon which Jesus has promised to build His church. The church is not built upon any mortal or any program. It is built upon the truth of the revelation of Jesus Christ.

That is why no man can say, "This is my church. I've given my money to it. I can control it." Only Jesus can say "This is My church. I have paid the price for it, and it is under My authority."

The mission of the church is implied in Jesus' words that "the gates of Hades shall not prevail against it" and the reference to the "keys of the kingdom of heaven." Sometimes we worry that Satan can prevail against the church. But Jesus announced that the church is His offensive weapon attacking Satan's strongholds of sin. The gates of Hades cannot keep the church from winning the lost, establishing justice, and manifesting holiness in the world.

The "keys" are the divine authority Christ has given the church in prayer and proclamation. In prayer, we discern what the Father's will is in the heavenlies. Through proclamation and other acts of obedience, we move forward in this world in the power of the Spirit so that His will is done on earth as it is in heaven (Matthew 6:10).

The book of Acts reveals the church in action. It is a church offering a new way to live. It is not self-serving but serving others. Christians are people who really do not "own" their possessions. The possessions we have are gifts of God for us to use for the purposes of His kingdom.

2. The Body of Christ
(1 Corinthians 12:12-27; Ephesians 3:1-12)

1 Corinthians 12:12 For as the body is one and has many members, but all the members of that one body, being many, are one body, so also is Christ.

13 For by one Spirit we were all baptized into one body — whether Jews or Greeks, whether slaves or free — and have all been made to drink into one Spirit.

14 For in fact the body is not one member but many.

15 If the foot should say, "Because I am not a hand, I am not of the body," is it therefore not of the body?

16 And if the ear should say, "Because I am not an eye, I am not of the body," is it therefore not of the body?

17 If the whole body were an eye, where would be the hearing? If the whole were hearing, where would be the smelling?

18 But now God has set the members, each one of them, in the body just as He pleased.

19 And if they were all one member, where would the body be?

20 But now indeed there are many members, yet one body.

21 And the eye cannot say to the hand, "I have no need of you"; nor again the head to the feet, "I have no need of you."

22 No, much rather, those members of the body which seem to be weaker are necessary.

23 And those members of the body which we think to be less honorable, on these we bestow greater honor; and our unpresentable parts have greater modesty,

24 but our presentable parts have no need. But God composed the body, having given greater honor to that part which lacks it,

25 that there should be no schism in the body, but that the members should have the same care for one another.

26 And if one member suffers, all the members suffer with it; or if one member is honored, all the members rejoice with it.

27 Now you are the body of Christ, and members individually.

Ephesians 3:1 For this reason I, Paul, the prisoner of Christ Jesus for you Gentiles —

2 if indeed you have heard of the dispensation of the grace of God which was given to me for you,

3 how that by revelation He made known to me the mystery (as I have briefly written already,

4 by which, when you read, you may understand my knowledge in the mystery of Christ),

5 which in other ages was not made known to the sons of men, as it has now been revealed by the Spirit to His holy apostles and prophets:

6 that the Gentiles should be fellow heirs, of the same body, and partakers of His promise in Christ through the gospel,

7 of which I became a minister according to the gift of the grace of God given to me by the effective working of His power.

8 To me, who am less than the least of all the saints, this grace was given, that I should preach among the Gentiles the unsearchable riches of Christ,

9 and to make all see what is the fellowship of the mystery, which from the beginning of the ages has been hidden in God who created all things through Jesus Christ;

10 to the intent that now the manifold wisdom of God might be made known by the church to the principalities and powers in the heavenly places,

11 according to the eternal purpose which He accomplished in Christ Jesus our Lord,

12 in whom we have boldness and access with confidence through faith in Him.

Although the church should be organized, it is not an organization. The church is the body, the living organism, of the Lord Jesus Christ. He is the head of the church, and the church is only empowered by His life, manifested in the Holy Spirit.

While there are many Christian denominations (human organizations meeting targeted needs and groups of people), there is only one body of Christ to which all Christian denominations and individuals belong. Within a local congregation, all believers are equally valuable in the place and gifts God has given them.

The fact that we are members of the one body of Christ is the basis for our love, understanding, support, and care for one another. That is why we should not be jealous of another member of the Body who receives blessings and recognition. His blessing is our blessing as members of Christ's body.

Paul discussed spiritual gifts within the context of the body of Christ and love (1 Corinthians 12, 13). While some gifts are more evident, every gift and every person are called by God. We honor the Lord as we honor, respect, and love one another.

3. The Great Commission
(Matthew 28:18-20)

Matthew 28:18 And Jesus came and spoke to them, saying, "All authority has been given to Me in heaven and on earth.

19 "Go therefore and make disciples of all the nations, baptizing them in the name of the Father and of the Son and of the Holy Spirit,

20 "teaching them to observe all things that I have commanded you; and lo, I am with you always, even to the end of the age." Amen.

It is appropriate that this study of church doctrine conclude with the Great Commission. As in the letters of Paul, doctrine serves to establish the basis for mission. Its mission is rooted in God's heart expressed in the Gospel. Anointed ministry flows from this basis into the world.

We are called to make disciples of those who respond to Christ. A disciple is a follower of Jesus. Because Jesus is the way, the truth, and the life, it is only right that we lead others to follow Him (John 14:6). Discipleship includes baptism and teaching. *Water baptism* is the public evidence that a sinner has been born again and belongs to Christ. It is a statement to the world and to the local church that this person is a follower of the Lord. *Teaching* includes cognitive knowledge as well as practical Christian living as a new creature in Christ. It is the impartation of truth that the Holy Spirit uses in our lives to conform us to the image of Christ.

Global Outreach Emphasis

The church is Christ's body on earth and is called to fulfill the Great Commission. We are Christ's body continuing the work that He began during His earthly ministry. He has given us the Holy Spirit, who leads us into all truth and gives us power to do "greater works" than Christ did (John 14:12-14).

This is why we place so much emphasis on world evangelism and Christian discipleship. These two go hand-in-hand as we fulfill the commandment of the Lord.

Word Power
RESPONSIBILITIES TO THE LOCAL CHURCH:

- *Leadership:* Christ has given His church leadership gifts of apostle, prophet, evangelist, and pastor-teachers. We show honor to Christ as we honor and respect these leaders (Hebrews 13:7, 17). We pray for our leaders, we submit to their authority in the Lord, and we use the gifts God has given us to help them accomplish God's will in a given situation and generation.

- ***Spiritual Gifts:*** Christ has given every believer one or more ministry gifts to be used in His Body. We use these with an attitude of reverence and love for Christ.
- ***Finances:*** The biblical model of financial support of a local church is tithing, that is, giving ten percent of one's income to the local church. Tithes are not ours to designate but are given so the local church can achieve its ordained purpose. We tithe obediently so that God will open the windows of heaven and pour forth the blessing He desires upon His people (Malachi 3:8-10).

  We give to special offerings (missions, education, special speakers, benevolence, etc.) above our tithes and do so with the heart of a cheerful giver (2 Corinthians 8, 9:7).
- ***Attendance:*** Hebrews 10:25 admonishes us not to forsake the assembling of ourselves together in worship and exhortation. We attend church services to be encouraged, built up, worship God, and fellowship with one another in Christian love. From such services, we are equipped better to serve Christ. Many of our gifts can be used in the local congregation to teach, serve in various capacities, sing, pray. Many of our gifts are to be used in the world as ways of reaching a dying world for the Living Lord.
- ***Unity:*** The previous four areas are related to this final section. Jesus prayed that His followers "may be one" (John 17:21-23). This unity is based on the divine unity existing between the Father and Son (17:21). This unity exists for the revelation and manifestation of God's love for a lost world. Our unity in the church is not a man-made unity demanding will-less submission and mindless obedience. Rather, it is a spiritual understanding of our relationships with other Christians. These relationships are not based upon worldly factors such as whether or not we "like" someone. Rather, these relationships are founded on Christ's love for all people. This unity demonstrates the truth of Jesus' words, "A new commandment I give to you, that you love one another; as I have loved you, that you also love one another. By this all will know that you are My disciples, if you have love for one another" (John 13:34, 35).

Bibliography

Brooks, Noel. "Studies on the Christian Doctrine of Salvation." *The Pentecostal Holiness Advocate*. Volume 61, No. 8-9 – Volume 63, No. 17. August 14, 1977 – December 23, 1979.

_____. *Scriptural Holiness*. Franklin Springs, Georgia: Advocate Press (now LifeSprings Resources), 1967.

_____. *Sickness, Health and God*. Franklin Springs, Georgia: Advocate Press (now LifeSprings Resources), 1965.

Brown, Francis, S.R. Driver and Charles A. Briggs. *A Hebrew and English Lexicon of the Old Testament*. Oxford: The Clarendon Press, 1968 edition.

Cooper, John W. *Body, Soul, and Life Everlasting: Biblical Anthropology and Monism-Dualism Debate*. Grand Rapids, Michigan: William B. Eerdmans Publishing Company, 1989.

Dieter, Melvin E. "The Wesleyan View." *Five Views On Sanctification*. Grand Rapids, Michigan: Zondervan Publishing House, 1987.

Erikson, Millard J. *Christian Theology*. Grand Rapids, Michigan: Baker Book House, 1985.

Fee, Gordon. *1 and 2 Timothy, Titus* in the *New Intermediate Biblical Commentary*, Peabody, Massachusetts: Hendrickson Publishers, 1988.

George, Timothy. "Luther's Theology." *Christian History*. Volume 34, 1995.

Henry, Carl F. *Revelation and the Bible*. London: The Tyndale Press, 1969.

Kepler, Thomas. *The Table Talk of Martin Luther*. Grand Rapids, Michigan: Baker Book House, 1952.

Kung, Hans. *Does God Exist? An Answer for Today*. New York, NY: Vintage Books, 1981.

Leith, John H. *Creeds of the Churches*. New York, NY: Doubleday Anchor, 1963.

Leith, John H. *From Generation to Generation: The Renewal of the Church According to Its Own Theology and Practice* Louisville, Kentucky: Westminster, John Knox Press, 1990.

Luther, Martin. *Luther's Works*. Vol. 1, *Genesis 1-5*. Edited and translated by Jaroslav Pelikan. St. Louis, Missouri: Concordia Publishing House, 1958.

_____. *Luther's Works*. Vol. 2. *Genesis 6-11*. Edited and translated by Jaroslav Pelikan. St. Louis, Missouri: Concordia Publishing House, 1958.

_____. *Luther's Works.* Vol. 48. Edited and translated by Jaroslav Pelikan. Philadelphia, Pennsylvania: Fortress Press.

McDowell, Josh. *A Ready Defense.* Nashville, Tennessee: Thomas Nelson Publisher, 1993.

Nash, Ronald H. *The Word of God and the Mind of Man.* Grand Rapids, Michigan: Zondervan Publishing House, 1982.

Pike, Garnet E. *Receiving the Promise of the Father: How To Be Baptized in the Holy Spirit.* Franklin Springs, Georgia: LifeSprings Resources, 1997.

Schaeffer, Francis. "Genesis in Time and Space." *A Christian View of the Bible as Truth.* Vol. 2 of *The Complete Works of Francis A. Schaeffer.* Westchester, Illinois: Crossway Books, 1982.

Soltau, Henry W. *The Tabernacle, The Priesthood, and The Offerings.* Harrisburg, Pennsylvania: Christian Publications, Inc., 1965 reprint.

Sproul, R.C. *Faith Alone: The Evangelical Doctrine of Justification.* Grand Rapids, Michigan: Baker Books, 1995.

Synan, Joseph A. "Doctrinal Amplification." *The Manual of the International Pentecostal Holiness Church 1993-1997.* Franklin Springs, Georgia: LifeSprings Resources, 1993.

Torrey, R.A. *The Person and Work of the Holy Spirit.* Grand Rapids, Michigan: Zondervan Publishing House, 1910.

Underwood, Bernard E. *Spiritual Gifts: Ministries and Manifestations.* Franklin Springs, Georgia: Advocate Press (now LifeSprings Resources), 1984.

_____. *The Spirit's Sword – God's Infallible Book.* Franklin Springs, Georgia: Advocate Press (now LifeSprings Resources), 1969.

Vine, W.E. *Expository Dictionary of New Testament Words.* Old Tappan, New Jersey: Fleming H. Revell Company, 1940.

Wesley, John. *Plain Account of Christian Perfection.* Columbia, South Carolina: Way of Faith Publishing House, 1899.

Wesley, John. *Sermons On Several Occasions.* London: The Epworth Press, 1746.

Williams, J. Rodman. *Renewal Theology: God, the World & Redemption.* Vol. 1. Grand Rapids, Michigan: Academie Books, Zondervan Publishing House, 1988.

_____. *Renewal Theology: Salvation, the Holy Spirit, and Christian Living.* Vol. 2. Grand Rapids, Michigan: Academie Books, Zondervan Publishing House, 1990.

Name and Subject Index

Abraham .... p. 9
Agape .... p. 10
Apocrypha .... p. 39
Apocryphal .... p. 39
Apostles' Creed .... p. 21
Articles of Faith .... p. 5

Babel, Tower of ...... p. 82
Bible .... p. 31ff
  Inspired p.32ff
  Plenary p.33
  Redemption p.35ff
  Two Testaments .p.34ff
  Verbal p.33
Brooks, Noel
  .... p.14n,51,74,76n

Chesed .... p. 10
Chalcedon, Council.p. 21
Church .p. 109ff.,115,116
Cooper, John p.41
Constantinople,
  Council .... p. 29
Cranmer, Thomas...p. 21

David, King p.70

Eastern Church ...... p. 30
Erickson, Millard J.
  .... p. 48n
Elohim .... p. 12
Evangelism .... p. 29
  Great Commission
  .... p.114

Fall, The .... p. 70,93
Fee, Gordon .... p. 40n
Feuerbach .... p. 8
Freud .... p. 8

God
  Love .... p. 10,20
  Omnipresence .... p. 14
  Omniscience .... p. 14
  Spirit .... p. 13

Healing .... p. 93ff

Heaven p.42ff
Hell p.44ff
Henry, Carl F. p.40n
Holy Spirit .... p. 23ff
  Baptism of .... p. 81
  Comforter .... p. 28
  Fruit of, ... p. 89,90
  Gifts .... p. 29,87-89
  Great Schism .... p. 29
  Love .... p. 91
  Salvation p.55
  Spirit of God .... p. 24ff
  Spirit-filled life .. p. 85ff
  Tongues (Glossolalia)
  ...p. 82-84,86,91n,92n

Islam .... p. 8

Joel .... p. 78
Jesus Christ .... p. 15ff
  Body of, ... p.111-114
  Messiah .... p. 20
  Sanctification ...p.68,69
  Savior .... p. 19ff
  Second Coming
  .... p. 101ff
    Imminent .... p. 101
    Personal .... p. 102
    Premillennial
    .... p. 102
  Son of God p.16ff,96
  Son of Man .... p. 18ff
Judaism .... p. 8
Judgment .... p. 47

Kung, Hans .... p. 14n

Leith, John ...... p. 6n,22n
Lewis, C.S. p.16,45
Life after death ..... p. 41ff
Luther, Martin
  .... p. 12,16,61,65,66

Marx .... p. 8
McDowell, Josh p.40n
Monotheism .... p. 8
Nash, Ronald p.40n

Nicene Creed ...... p. 21,29

Old Testament .... p. 9

Pentecost ...... p. 77ff.,85ff
Propitiation .... p. 21ff
Pseudepigrapha ...... p. 39

Revelation, Book of
  .... p. 107,108

Salvation .... p. 49ff
  Atonement..p. 93,96,97
  Born Again
  (Regeneration)
  .... p.51ff.,68,74
  Deliverance from sin
  .... p.53ff
  Faith...p. 28,56,60ff,63,
  69,74,75,98,100
  Forgiveness of sins
  .... p.50ff
  Good Works p.62ff
  Justification ...p.57ff,68
  Objective p.55
  Remission p.51
  Righteousness .... p. 58ff
  Sanctification
  ...... p.55,56,67ff,73,74
  Definite
  instantaneous ...p. 74
  Received by faith
  .... p. 74
  Subjective .... p. 55
Satan .... p. 8,28
Schaeffer, Francis
  .... p.14n,38,40n
Shema .... p. 9
Sin .... p. 69,72
Soltau, Henry p.21
Sproul, R.C., ... p.66n
Synan, J.A. .... p. 23,30n

Temptation .... p. 72
Ten Commandments p. 9
Thirty-Nine Articles....p. 21

Torrey, R.A..............p. 25
Trinity......p. 11,12,29,84

Underwood, B.E.
................p.40n,92n

Wesley, John
......p.33,68,70-72,76n
Williams, Rodman
...............p. 10,14n,59

Vine, W.E. p.51

Scripture Index

Genesis
1:2   p. 24,25
1:26   p. 12,13
3   p. 93
11   p.82
11:7   p. 12
15:6   p.64
17:1   p. 14
20:17,18   p.93
21:1,2   p.93
22:1-19   p.64

Exodus
3:1-5   p.81
15:11   p. 14
15:23-25   p.93
20:1-6   p. 9
23:16   p.80
25:17-22   p. 22
34:6   p. 14
34:22   p.80

Leviticus
16:2,11-15   p. 22
23:15-22   p.80

Numbers
21:6-9   p.93
23:19   p. 14
28:26-31   p.80

Deuteronomy
4:35   p. 9
5:6-10   p. 9
6:4,5   p. 8, 9
16:9-12   p.80

Joshua
3:10   p. 13

2 Samuel
11,12   p.71

1 Kings
13:6   p.93
17:17-24   p. 93

2 Kings
2:21,22   p. 93
4:32-37   p. 93
5   p.100

Psalms
2:7,8   p. 16
19:1-6   p. 7
32:2   p.59
51   p.70
51:5-7,10   p. 71
99:4   p. 14
103:4,8   p. 14
103:12   p.51
104:24   p. 14
106:1   p. 14
139:7-10   p. 14

Proverbs
8:22-31   p. 25

Ecclesiastes
3:11   p.41

Isaiah
2:8,17,20,21   p. 9
4:4   p. 25
11:1,2   p. 24
19:20   p. 19
40:18-23,25   p. 9
40:28   p. 13,14
42:8   p. 7
43:25   p.51
44:6,8   p. 9
53   p.19
53:4,5   p.96,97
53:5   p.93
61:1-3   p.26,27

Jeremiah
2:4,5   p. 9
10:1-10   p. 9
23:23,24   p. 14

Ezekiel
36:29   p.71

Daniel
2:20,21   p. 14
7:13,14   p. 18

Joel
2   p.80
2:28-32   p.78

Malachi
3:8-10   p.116

Matthew
1:21   p. 20
3:1-12   p.81
3:13-17   p.81
3:16,17   p. 11
4:1-11   p.72
5:16   p.63
5:22   p.48
5:44,45   p. 14
6:10   p.111
8:16,17   p.97
10:28   p.48
12:31   p. 25
16:16   p.111
16:18,19   p.110
19:28   p.44
24:3-14   p.102,103
24:27-31   p.104,105
24:44   p.101
25:31   p. 43
26:28   p.50
28:18-20   p.114
28:19   p. 11

Mark
1:9-11   p. 16,17
1:40-45   p.93
3:1-6   p. 93
5:25-34   p. 93
9:31   p. 19
10:45   p. 19
12:29   p. 9
16:15   p.109

Luke
2:14 p. 43
8 p.96
8:43-48 p.94,95
13:10-17 p.93
16 p. 45
16:19-31 p.44,45
17:11-19 p.93
22:28-30 p.44

John
3:3-8 p.52
3:8 p.80
3:16 p. 14,49
3:36 p.41,46
4:23, 24 p. 24
4:24 p. 13
4:42 p. 20
5:1-18 p.93
5:39 p.35
6:57 p. 13
6:63,68 p.35
9:3 p.99
10:32 p.63
13:34, 35 p.116
14:1-6 p.42, 43
14:3 p.43
14,15,16 p. 28
14:6 p. 15,115
14:12-14 p.115
14:16,17,25,26 p.26, 27
14:17 p. 25
15:26 p. 23,27
16:5-15 p.27
17:3 p. 13
17:17,19 p.68
17:21-23, p.116
17:25 p. 14

Acts
2 p.78,80,82
2:1-4 p.79
2:4 p.83
2:14 p.83
2:16-21 p.80
2:39 p.77
3 p.96
3:1-10 p.95
4:32-35 p.110
7:51 p. 25

8:14-19 p.83
9:17 p.83
10:38 p.63
10:44-47 p.83
13:1-4 p. 24,25
15:28 p. 25
16:6,7 p. 25
16:16-19 p.100
19:1-6 p.81,83
26:18 p.74
26:25 p.83

Romans
1:4 p. 25
1:17 p.65
1:20 p. 7,13
3:23 p.50
3:25 p. 22
3:28 p.61
4:5 p.59
4:8 p.59
4:13-25 p.58,59
5:1-11 p.60,61
5:1 p.57
5:5 p.28
5:8 p. 14
5:12-21 p.94
6:1-11 p.69,70
6:3 p.84n
6:11 p.71
6:11-16 p.53,54
6:15-23 p.71,72
8:2 p. 26
8:5-10 p.74
8:9 p. 25
8:19-22 p.94
8:26,27 p.87,92n
8:33,34 p.59
12:3-8 p. 29
12:6-8 p.87,88

1 Corinthians
1:30 p.68
2:10,11 p. 25
3:11-15 p.47
3:16 p.86
6:11 p.29
6:19 p.27,28,86
10:13 p.72
12 p.89,91,100,114

12:4-7 p. 29
12:11 p. 25
12:12-27 p.111,112
12:27-31 p.88
12:31 p.91
13 p.91,114
13:9-12 p.43
13:11-15 p.47
14 p.87,91
14:1 p.91
14:1-5 p.86
14:15 p.87
14:18 p.83
14:27,28 p.87
15:3,4 p. 21
15:35-49 p.56
16:22 p.101

2 Corinthians
3:3 p.25
3:18 p.56
4:7 p.90
5:9,10 p.47
5:17 p.53
5:18 p.22
5:19 p.59
5:21 p.59
7:2 p.71
8 p.116
9:7 p.116
12:2-4 p.43
13:14 p. 11

Galatians
2:20 p.74
4:6 p. 25
5 p.90
5:22-25 p.89, 90
5:25 p.85

Ephesians
1:6,7 p. 14
1:7 p.50
1:13 p. 25,84n
1:14 p.28,84n
2:1-10 p.51,52
2:1,5 p.53
2:8-10 p.63
2:10 p.63
3:1-12 p.112,113

4 p.89	10:14 p.69	21 p.106
4:4-6 p.84n	10:23 p. 6	21:3 p.43
4:11-16 p.88	10:25 p.116	21:4 p.43
4:22 p.70	10:29 p. 26	22 p.106
4:22,25-31 p.70	12:22-24 p.44	
4:30 p.25	13:7,17 p.115	
5:25-27 p.74	13:11,12 p.74	

Philippians
1:19 p. 25
2:9,10   p.48

Colossians
1:14 p.50
1:15 p. 13
2:2,3 p. 14
3:5-11   p.70

1 Thessalonians
4:15-18   p.106
5:2-4   p.106

2 Thessalonians
2:1-12 p.103,104
2:10,12 p.104
2:13   p.69

2 Timothy
2:13 p. 14
3:16 p. 31,34
3:16,17   p. 6,32
3:17 p.34

Titus
2:11 p. 14
2:14 p.74

Hebrews
1:9 p. 26
2:11 p.68
2:17 p. 22
2:18 p.72
3:11,18 p.43
4:9-11 p.43
4:12 p.34
4:13 p. 14
4:15,16 p.72
9:5   p. 22
9:13,14   p.74
10:10,14-22 p.74

James
1:12-15 p.72
2:14-26 p.62,64
2:21 p.64
3:6 p.48
5:13-16   p. 98

1 Peter
1:15,16 p. 14,67
2:24,25   p.97
4:14 p. 26

2 Peter
1:19-21 p.34,35
2:4   p. 48
3:10-14   p.106, 107

1 John
1:7-9 p.68,71
1:9 p.51
2:2 p.22,50
2:18,21-23 p. 16,17
3:2   p.43
3:7-9 p.54
4:7-21 p. 9,10,13
4:10   p. 22
5:4,5,10-13 p. 16,17
5:7   p. 11

Jude
24   p.73

Revelation
5:1-7   p.108
6:1   p.108
6-19 p.108
19:1-4   p.44
19:6   p. 14
19:11-16   p.105
20:4,6 p.47,106
20:7-10   p.106
20:11-15   p. 47,106